AF522615

RURAL ECONOMY

CHANGING LANDSCAPE

RURAL ECONOMY
CHANGING LANDSCAPE

Editor
Dr. Kartick Das
Teacher-in-Charge
Samuktala Sidhu Kanhu College
Samuktala
Alipurduar District
West Bengal - 735 121
(INDIA)

Published by:

Namit Wasan

DISCOVERY PUBLISHING HOUSE PVT. LTD.
4383/4B, Ansari Road, Darya Ganj
New Delhi - 110 002 (India)
Phone : +91-11-23279245, 43596064-65
Fax : +91-11-23253475
E-mail : discoverypublishinghouse@gmail.com
namitwasan9@gmail.com
sales@discoverypublishinggroup.com
web : www.discoverypublishinggroup.com

***First Edition:* 2017**

ISBN: 978-93-5056-838-5

Rural Economy: ***Changing Landscape***

Printed at:
Infinity Imaging Systems
Delhi

Dedicated with Admiration to My Father

Late Sibu Das

(15-09.1939 – 08.11.2014)

Preface & Acknowledgement

This volume contains 10 research papers is the outcome of the research findings of academicians and researchers of different disciplines. Its throw light on various dimensions of higher education in India. It tries to explore the present condition and analysis of past development experiences in the higher education sector and will propose new initiatives to address the needs of the higher education sector. Further the book will looks in detail at the issues of access, equity and excellence in the Indian higher education system.

I am extremely grateful to all the contributors for their scholarly contributions to make this volume a useful addition to the existing body of literature on the subject. I would like to express my sincere thanks and gratitude to Dr. P.K. Sengupta, Professor of Political Science, University of North Bengal, for his constant guidance and encouragement to work and publish literatures in the field of higher education. I wish to place on record my profound thanks to my teacher Prof. Nibash Paul, Lumding College, Lumding, Assam, who motivated and supported me directly or indirectly to do so. I must also express my hearty gratitude to all staff members of Samuktala Sidhu Kanhu College, Samuktala, Alipurduar, West Bengal for their inspiring attitude. Finally, I acknowledge with thanks the co-operation and help extended to me by my wife Mithu Sarkar Das, Assistant Teacher and my two sons, Sagar Shekhar and Aakashnil, for being very supportive kids.

– Kartick Das

Contents

Contributors

1. **Dr. S. Vijay Kumar**, Head and Associate Professor (Retd.), Department of Economics, Kakatiya Government (UG&PG) College, Hanamkonda, Warangal District, Telangana.
2. **Dr. Kartick Das**, Teacher-in-Charge, Samuktala Sidhu Kanhu College, Alipurduar, West Bengal.
3. **Milan Banik**, Assistant Professor, Department of Economics, Rukasen College, Bakalia, Karbi Anglong, Assam.
4. **Dr. Biju K.C.,** Assistant Professor, Department of Economics, St. Thomas College, Palai, Arunapuram PO: Kottayam, Dt., Kerala, India.
5. **Sudipta Biswas**, Programme Manager, Rural Development Institute, West Bengal.
6. **Dr. Vijayalakshmi Kanteti**, Professor and Principal, St. Xaviers P.G. College, Hyderabad, Telangana.
7. **Dr. Sanjay Kanti Das,** Assistant Professor and Head, Department of Commerce, Lumding College, Lumding, Nagaon, Assam.
8. **Dr. Rathindra Nath Pramanik,** Associate Professor (Economics), PalliCharcha Kendra, Department Rural Studies, Visva-Bharati, Sriniketan, West Bengal.
9. **Anil Kumar Biswas,** Assistant Professor, Department of Political Science, University of Burdwan, Burdwan, West Bengal.

Abbreviations

ADB	-	Asian Development Bank.
ADD	-	Attention Deficit Disorder.
AIC	-	Agriculture Insurance Company.
AIDIS	-	All India Debt and Investment Survey.
AP	-	Andhra Pradesh.
ASP	-	Application Service Provider.
BC	-	Business Correspondent.
BPL	-	Below Poverty Line.
CABE	-	Central Advisory Board of Education.
CAGR	-	Compound Annual Growth Rate.
CB	-	Commercial Banks.
CBS	-	Core Banking Solution.
CCB	-	Central Cooperative Bank.
CCE	-	Crop Cutting Experiment.
CCIS	-	Comprehensive Crop Insurance Scheme.
CCT	-	Conditional Cash Transfers.
CD	-	Community Development CD: Credit-Deposit.
CEO	-	Chief Executive Officer.
CMIE	-	Centre for Monitoring Indian Economy.
CSA	-	Co-operative Societies Act.
CSMS	-	Core Subsidy Management System.
CSS	-	Centrally Sponsored Scheme.
DICGC	-	Deposit Insurance and Credit Guarantee Corporation.
DISE	-	District Information System for Education.
DONER	-	Ministry of Development of North Eastern Region.
DPEP	-	District Primary Education Programme.
DRDA	-	District Rural Development Agency.
DRDC	-	District Rural Development Cell.
DVA	-	Domestic Violence Act.

EDI	-	Educational Development Index.
FCIC	-	Federal Crop Insurance Corporation.
FYP	-	Five-Year Plan.
GDP	-	Gross Domestic Product.
GEI	-	Gender Equality Index.
GER	-	Gross Enrolment Ratio.
GHG	-	Green House Gas.
GIC	-	General Insurance Corporation.
GIPSA	-	General Insurance Public Sector Association.
GLC	-	Ground Level Credit.
GoI	-	Government of India.
GPI	-	Gender Parity Index.
HDR	-	Human Development Report.
HEI	-	Higher Education Institutions.
HRD	-	Human Resource Development.
IARI	-	Indian Agriculture Research Institute.
ICB	-	Institutional Capacity Building.
ICESCR	-	International Covenant on Economic, Social and Cultural Rights.
ICOR	-	Incremental Capital-Output Ratio.
ICT	-	Information and Communication Technology.
IDSK	-	Institute of Development Studies.
IEDC	-	Integrated education for Disabled Children.
ILO	-	International Labour Organization.
IMD	-	Indian Meteorological Department.
IMR	-	Infant Mortality Rate.
IPDSS	-	Institutional Protection and Deposit Safety Scheme.
IRDP	-	Integrated Rural Development Programme.
JLG	-	Joint Liability Group.
KCC	-	Kisan Credit Card.
KGVB	-	Kasturba Gandhi Balika Vidyalaya.
KYC	-	Know Your Customer.
LTCCS	-	Long Term Cooperative Credit Structure.
MCI	-	Mutual Crop Insurance.
MCII	-	Mutual Crop Income Insurance.

MDG	-	Millennium Development Goal.
MDMS	-	Mid Day Meal Scheme.
MFI	-	Micro-Finance Institutions.
MIS	-	Management Information System.
MNAIS	-	Modified National Agriculture Insurance Scheme.
MNREGA	-	Mahatma Gandhi National Rural Employment Guarantee Act.
MoRD	-	Ministry of Rural Development.
MoU	-	Memorandum of Understanding.
MPCI	-	Multiple Peril Crop Insurance.
MSCSA	-	Multi State Co-operative Societies Act.
NSSO	-	National Sample Survey Organization.
NABARD	-	National Bank for Agriculture and Rural Development.
NABFINS	-	NABARD Financial Services.
NAIS	-	National Agriculture Insurance Scheme.
NBFC	-	Non-Banking Financial Company.
NCDC	-	National Co-operative Development Corporation.
NCLP	-	National Child Labour Project.
NEC	-	North Eastern Council.
NGO	-	Non-Governmental Organization.
NIA	-	National Insurance Academy.
NLM	-	National Literacy Mission.
NMFL	-	National Mission for Female Literacy.
NPE	-	National Policy on Education.
NREGA	-	National Rural Employment Guarantee Act.
NREP	-	National Rural Employment Programme.
NRHM	-	National Rural Health Mission.
NRLM	-	National Rural Livelihood Mission.
NSSO	-	National Sample Survey Organization.
PACS	-	Primary Agricultural Credit Societies.
PCIS	-	Pilot Crop Insurance Scheme.
PMGS	-	Pradhan Mantri Gram Sadak Yojana.
PSF	-	Price Stabilisation Fund.
RBI	-	Reserve Bank of India.
RCI	-	Rehabilitation Council of India.

RCS - Registrar Co-operative Societies.
RFID - Radio Frequency Identification.
RGGVY - Rajib Gandhi Grameen Vidyutikaran Yojana.
RMK - Rastriya Mahila Kosh.
RRB - Regional Rural Bank.
RSBY - Rastriya Swasthya Bima Yojana.
RTE - Right to Education.
RUSA - Rashtriya Uchchatar Shiksha Abhiyan.
S&M - Small and Marginal.
SC - Scheduled Caste.
SCB - State Co-operative Bank.
SF/MF - Small Farmer/Marginal Farmer.
SFDA - Small Farmer Development Agency.
SFDs - Special Focus Districts.
SGSY - Swaranjayanti Gram Swarazagar Yojana.
SHG - Self-Help Group.
SHPI - Self-Help Promotion Institution.
SNE - Special Need Education.
SSA - Sarva Shiksha Abhiyan
ST - Scheduled Tribe.
STCCS - Short-Term Co-operative Credit Structure.
SWOT - Strengths, Weakness, Opportunities and Threats.
TOPS - Terrestrial Observation and Protection System.
ToR - Terms of Reference.
TSU - Technical Support Unit.
UDHR - Universal Declaration of Human Rights.
ULBs - Urban Local Bodies.
UNCRPD - Convention on the Rights of Persons with Disabilities.
UNDP - United Nations Development Programme.
UNESCO - United Nations Educational, Scientific and Cultural Organization.
UNGA - UN General Assembly.
UPA - United Progressive Alliance.
VE&T - Vocational Education and Training.
WBCIS - Weather risk-Based Crop Insurance Scheme.
WG - Working Group.

Pages: 1-7

Rural Economy: *Changing Landscape*
Edited by: **Dr. Kartick Das**
ISBN: 978-93-5056-838-5
Edition: **2017**
Published by: **Discovery Publishing House Pvt. Ltd., New Delhi (India)**

Improving Infrastructure
Changing Rural Landscape

— **Kartick Das**

A nation's infrastructure development plays a significant role in its economic growth. A fast-growing economy warrants an even faster development of infrastructure. It is generally recognised that lack of infrastructure is one of the major constraints on India's ability to achieve 9 to 10 per cent growth in Gross Domestic Product (GDP), which is the rate required to make growth more inclusive and make a significant difference to living conditions of 800 million strong rural population of the country. For the balance growth of any economy, rural sector needs equal attention if not more than that of its urban counterpart.

Bharat Nirman – Gateway to India's Prosperity

The government's flagship programmes have been the principal instrumental for implementing its agenda for inclusive development. Improvement in rural infrastructure is crucial for broad-based inclusive growth of the economy and for bridging the rural-urban divide. The special programme, Bharat Nirman with its six schemes for up-gradation of rural infrastructure, launched in 2005, aims to provide electricity to the remaining 1,25,000 villages and to 23 million households; to connect the remaining 66,802 habitations with all weather roads; to construct 1,46,185 km., of new rural roads network; to provide drinking water to 55,067 uncovered habitations; to provide irrigation to an additional 10 million hectares; and to connect the remaining 66,822 villages with telephones.

Rural Mural: At A Glance

- The growth in India's rural areas is spurred by improved infrastructure that enables reach, awareness of brands and a steady growth in household income that in turn grows consumption.
- Rural India accounts for 55 per cent of India's total income.
- The rural market is bigger than urban for FMCG, durables, two-wheelers companies and several services as well.
- Rural India contributes 40 per cent auto sales.
- Women in rural India have got empowered through the five million micro finance groups with 50 million women members.
- Traditional rural income sources from framing now changing to non-farm sector.
- Healthcare, education and construction are the fastest growing sectors in rural India.
- Women in rural India have got empowered through the five million micro finance groups with 50 million women members.

- Studies conducted by Planning Commission and elsewhere have shown that the Pradhan Mantri Gram Sadak Yojana (PMGSY) roads have resulted in significant benefits to rural households because of better connectivity to markets and also easier access to health and educational facilities.
- PMGSY is one of the most successful programmes under Bharat Nirman which provides all weather road connectivity to rural habitations with a population of 500 persons and above 250 persons and above in respect of hill states, the tribal and the desert areas with an all weather road.
- Dramatic improvement has also been evident in sanitation through Accelerated Irrigation Benefit Programme. The coverage of rural households provided with individual latrines has improved sharply from 27.0 per cent in 2004 to 62.0 per cent in 2011.
- Under Rajib Gandhi Grameen Vidyutikaran Yojana, Ministry of Power has sanctioned 568 projects for 540 districts to electrify 118,533 villages and to provide free electricity connections to 2.46 Crore BPL rural households. As on 31st August 2009, 64,331 villages have been electrified and 68.97 lakh free electricity connections have been released to BPL households.

- Under National Rural Drinking Water Programme, 55,067 habitations uncovered and about 3.31 lakh slipped-back habitations and 2.17 lakh quality-affected habitations have been covered with provisions of drinking water facilities by end of 2011.
- Telecom connectivity constitutes an important part of the effort to upgrade the rural infrastructure. Cellular mobile telephone revolution has connected urban as well as rural India. Tele density has increased from 0.7 per cent in 2001 to 23 per cent in 2011. Telephone subscribers in India increased from 0.5 million in 1991 to 862 million by June 2011.
- A total of 2.4 crore families have been covered under Rashtriya Swasthya Bima Yojana and over 8,600 health care providers are enrolled in the selected districts across 29 States and Union Territories.

Improving Rural Infrastructure
(Narrowing Rural Urban Divide)

Rural Share of Wallet		Urban Share of Wallet	
Food beverages	55	Food beverages	45
Housing	4	Housing	6
Health	5	Health	5
Transport	10	Transport	11
Education	6	Education	9
Clothing	7	Clothing	7
Durables	5	Durables	5
Others	8	Others	12

Source: Max-NCAER, 2007.

Improving Infrastructure
(Changing Landscape)

Infrastructure	2001	2010
Tele density	0.7	21
Road connectivity in villages	40	70
Electrified Households	44	60+
Permanent Houses	41	56

Figures in percentage, *Source:* Economic Survey FY11.

Population and Consumption

Population		Consumption	
Rural	70%	Rural	57%
Urban	30%	Urban	43%

Source: UN Population Statistics and NSS.

Issues of Concern

India's current rural infrastructure deficit is alarming. Despite the aggressive growth in the last few years, India's basic infrastructure ranked 86 in the Global Competitive Rank.

- The rural electrification programme, launched in 1951, has succeeded in bringing electricity to more than 5 lakh villages. However, 80,000 villages are yet to get electricity connections.
- RGGVY focuses only on household supply and does not address the need for providing electricity for agriculture.
- In spite of a significant expansion of telecom sector, however, India's rural tele-density remains appallingly low.
- India possesses 16 per cent of the world's population but just 4 per cent of its water resources. A large number of rural habitations remain without any identified source of safe drinking water.
- Along with water quality, poor sanitation is one of the factors contributing to malnutrition.
- A major weakness of the IAY has been the quality of housing. There have been complaints about weak foundations, poor roofing materials and incomplete constructions.
- There are significant regional imbalances in the connectivity of villages. Lack of maintenance of roads is a major problem in India.

The India's GDP was $1.4 trillion at the end of March 2011. Today India is the second fastest growing economics of the world, yet ranks low in comparison to world standards in infrastructure financing, spending only about 8 per cent of GDP as compared to China where they spend as high as 20 per cent of the GDP. During the 11th Five-year Plan investment in infrastructure sector fell short of its target of $500 billion. In order to maintain sustainable growth, investment in infrastructure would need to increase further. The government of India has identified infrastructure investment as route of sustained economic recovery and the key driver of economic growth. The government has announced a serous of measures for infra-financing, including an

$11 million debt-fund, in line with its target to doubling investment to $1 trillion over the 12th Five-year Plan (at 2006-07 prices). To generate $1 trillion for infra-financing by 2012-17, roughly the size of its current GDP, this would imply an annual infrastructure investment of $200 billion – a truly challenging one.

Projected Investment under 12th Plan ($ Billion)

2012-13	2013-14	2014-15	2015-16	2016-17
155	178	202	229	260

Source: Approach Paper, 12th Five-year Plan, GOI.

Priorities: The Task Ahead

In the above context, this investment has to be divided into centre, states and private sectors. Despite continued emphasis on public-private partnership (PPP) model as an alternative route of developing and financing infrastructure, but the participation of public-private investment has been dismally low. Private investment could be improved if investors find it profitable and reasonable since infra-projects are typically characterised by non-recourse or limited-recourse financing and low and risk-adjusted returns. Keeping user charges low is only feasible way to improve infra-financing and therefore government have to bear some of the capital cost in the form of a capital subsidy as in road project where government allowed up to 40 per cent of the capital cost as a subsidy. Infrastructure development has been localized to an extent and needs to spread all over to provide a holistic growth to India's economy.

Road Ahead – Vision 2020

(Based on Report of the Committee on India Vision 2020, Planning Commission, GOI)

Core Areas	Present	2020
Power capacity	1,85,496 mw	2,60,496 mw
National Highway	71,772 km	85,000 km
Expressway	2,600 km	18,637 km
Two-lane road	9,220 km	15,000 km
Ports capacity	1,240 mt	3,130 mt
Route network	64,000 km	89,000 km
Aircraft	400	1000
Air passengers	142 million	450 million

For realizing Vision 2020 in infrastructure sector, reforms needed at various levels. The Government of India should emphasise policies to revitalised flow of capital in infrastructure like: initiating tax free bond, encouraging public-private partnership, by liberalizing the country's FDI policy, by increasing FII investment limits in corporate bonds, etc. With these, other obstacles such as: delay in land acquisition, environmental clearances, slow approvals from government department are to be address precisely.

- A PPP model seems to be the way out to meet challenges of increasing demands of rural infrastructure. The state, the industry and private entrepreneurs working together through PPP model will be ideal way out to upgrade and modify rural infrastructure as it would be unrealistic to completely rely on public or private investments.
- India would require developing a rupee-denominated long-term bond market for funding the infrastructure sector.
- There is a need to reduce over-reliance on the banking system for infrastructure funding. For this, a strong focus is required to develop a deep and robust corporate bond market. Companies should be allowed to float and trade corporate bonds for infra-related project purposes. The India Infrastructure Debt Fund with an initial corpus of Rs. 50,000 crore dedicated for infrastructure makes ample sense, given the sheer shortage of long-term project finance.
- The relevance of the India Infrastructure Financial Company Limited (IIFCL), set up to provide long-term financial assistance, needs to be reviewed. IIFCL is an enticing but flawed financial engineering mechanism.
- To accelerate growth, India needs to create a pipeline of PPP project and create long-term sources of financing with pension funds flows into infrastructure instead of only bank funds.

Summing Up

Despite of the relative satisfactory performance in some of the macro-economic variables and spending thousands of crores of rupees for rural infrastructural programmes aimed at improving the nation's social indicators, large part of the rural population still lack access to basic services in health, education, clean drinking water, sanitation and housing. The problem of rural infrastructure cannot be viewed or tackled in isolation from changes affecting the urban landscape. A comprehensive and integrated strategy is required. The natural growth of urban areas will make this trend inevitable unless bold steps are taken to promote an alternative, more geographically dispersed and equitable development paradigm.

Pages: 8-56

Rural Economy: ***Changing Landscape***
Edited by: **Dr. Kartick Das**
ISBN: 978-93-5056-838-5
Edition: **2017**
Published by: **Discovery Publishing House Pvt. Ltd., New Delhi (India)**

2 MGNREGA in Rural Employment and Development
An Assessment

— Sanjay Kanti Das

INTRODUCTION

The National Rural Employment Guarantee Scheme (henceforth NREGS) is one of the most significant interventions of Government in the generation of rural employment in India. The NREGS is a landmark in the economic history of independent India which provides legal rights on employment to the rural citizens. The scheme, addressed especially to the problem of galloping rural unemployment, commands a position of an unparallel significance in amelioration of poverty and unemployment in the post-independent era. The NREGS is in fact, the manifestation of National Rural Employment Guarantee Act (henceforth NREGA) 2005 further renamed as Mahatma Gandhi National Rural Employment Guarantee Act (MGNREGA). The scheme is the bold and most pragmatic approach of the Government of India to rural unemployment which was ceremoniously launched on an all India basis in Bandlaplli village of Annantpur District of Andhra Pradesh on 2nd February, 2006. Initially, the Scheme covered 200 most backward districts having high percentage of SC and ST population. The Act is also a significant vehicle for strengthening decentralised and deepening process of democracy by giving a pivotal role to the *Panchayati Raj* Institutions concerning planning, monitoring and implementation. Unique feature of the Act include time bound employment guarantee within 15 days and incentive-disincentive structure to the State Governments for providing employment as 90 per cent of the cost for employment is borne by the Centre or payment of unemployment allowance at their own cost and emphasis on labour intensive works prohibiting the use of contractors and machinery. The Act also recommended 33 per cent participation for women.

The key objective of launching of MGNREGS is to uplift the backward socio-economic conditions of rural people of India. It indicates that the socio-economic backwardness of rural India has profound impact in launching of MGNREGS and therefore, the central Government has implemented the Scheme with a lot of enthusiasm. The major landmarks in the history of passing of such Act are represented as below.

Milestones of the Indian Journey towards MGNREGA

1952 Community Development Programme (CDP).

1960 Rural Manpower Programme (RMP).

1971 Crash Scheme for Rural Employment (CSRE).

1972 Intensive Rural Employment Programme (IREP) on Pilot basis.

1973 Small Farmers Development Agency (SFDA), Marginal Farmers and Agricultural Labour Scheme (MFAL).

1977 Food for Work Programme (FWP).

1980 National Rural Employment Programme (NREP).

1983 Rural Landless Employment Guarantee Programme (RLEGP).

1993 Jawahar Rozgar Yojana (JRY) and Employment Assurance Scheme (EAS).

1999 Jawahar Gram Samridhi Yojana (JGSY).

2001 Sampoorna Grameen Rozgar Yojana (SGRY).

2004 National Food for Work (NFFWP).

2005 Notification of NREGA.

2006 Implementation of Phase I - NREGA in 200 districts of India.

2007 Extension of Phase II - NREGA to additional 130 Districts.

2008 NREGA Phase III - Extended to cover all districts of India.

2009 NREGA renamed as Mahatma Gandhi National Rural Employment Guarantee Act (MNREGA) and extended whole country.

Source: History of Development and Employment Programmes in India: at a Glance. Available at http://tarunguptaiitian.wordpress.com/ias/187-2/

The significance of MGNREGA lies in the fact that it creates a right based framework for wage employment programme and makes the government legally bound to extend employment to those who demand it. While the Act provides a legal framework, the state governments have the legal liability and the central Government provides the fiscal guarantee. The Act ensures that there is decentralised planning, which means a perspective plan needs to be prepared for the whole district with a list of permissible works. In this way the legislation goes beyond providing a social safety net and towards guaranteeing the right to employment.

A national overview on the performance of MGNREGA in India is represented in Table 2.1 which depicts that in 2006-07, 3.78 crores job cards were issued which rose to 12.54 crores at the end of Dec., 2012. Further, 2.10 crores employment was generated in 2006-07 which further rose to 4.16 cores *i.e.,* near about double during the seven years of implementation. Similarly, 90.5 crores mandays of employments were provided to households in 2006-07 which is almost double in 2012-13.

Table 2.1: Performance of MGNREGA: A National Overview

Unique Feature	2006-07	2007-08	2008-09	2009-10	2010-11	2011-12	2012-13	2013-14*
Total Job Card issued [in Crore]	3.78	6.48	10.01	11.25	11.98	12.39	12.79	12.72
Employment provided to households [in Crore]	2.10	3.39	4.51	5.26	5.49	5.04	4.98	3.81
Person days [in Crore]	90.5	143.59	216.32	283.59	257.15	216.34	229.86	134.80

*Till 31st Dec, 2013; *Source*: Ministry of Rural Development, 2014.

On February 2, 2006 first phase of MGNREGA implementation was started in 200 districts of the country in which seven districts of Assam were also incorporated. In the year 2007, the second phase of MGNREGA had started where five districts of Assam were also included. The third phase started on April 1, 2008 where remaining 14 districts of Assam came within the purview of the Act. At present, all the districts of Assam are implementing the Scheme. On March 31, 2013 Assam completed seven years of MGNREGA implementation.

All together ten permissible varieties of works were taken up such as: rural connectivity, flood control, water conservation and water harvesting, drought proofing including afforestation and tree plantation, micro irrigation, provision of irrigation facility to land development, renovation of traditional water bodies, land development, any other activity approved by Ministry of Rural Development and work under *Bharat Nirman, Rajib Gandhi Seva Kendra* under MGNREGA. Among all the programmes, the scheme rural connectivity got top priority. It may be happened due to the prevailing poor road connectivity in the villages of Assam in particular and NER for which it assumed top priority among all the ongoing schemes under MGNREGA.

Table 2.2 depicts the percentage of expenditure incurred in the different heads of works undertaken under MGNREGA during 2012-13. The comparative analysis on major works undertaken under MGNREGA reveals that in India as a whole around 71 lakh works were undertaken (including new works as well as spill-over works from the previous year), of which 60 per cent relate to water conservation, 12 per cent for the provision of irrigation facility to land owned by SC/ST/BPL, IAY beneficiaries, small farmers or marginal farmers as defined in the Agriculture debt waiver and debt relief schemes or beneficiaries under the STs and other traditional forest dwellers (Recognition of forest right) Act 2006, 17 per cent rural connectivity and 8 per cent for land development in 2012-13 (up to Dec. 2012). Assam and other NER States also follow the similar pattern of projects under MGNREGS during 2012-13.

Table 2.2: Expenditure on Different Heads of Works, 2012-13 (in Percentage; up to Dec. 2012)

Major Works under MGNREGA	Assam	NER	India
Water conservation	11%	9%	60%
Provision of irrigation facility to land owned by SC/ST/BPL and IAY beneficiaries	32%	26%	12%
Rural connectivity	47%	52%	17%
Land development	1%	6%	8%
Any other activity including: Bharat Nirman, Rajiv Gandhi Seva Kendra, rural drinking water, fisheries etc.	9%	7%	3%

Source: Ministry of Rural Development, 2013.

It is reported by Ministry of Rural Development, 2013 that in the year 2011-12, Assam completed 9,970 numbers of projects by creating equal numbers of rural assets. Sonitpur district completed highest 2,163 numbers of work, whereas Chirang and Nalbari districts bottomed the list by completing one and seven works respectively in the whole year. It is also reported (NEST Report, 2013[1]) that out of ten categories of works approved in the MGNREGA, 62 per cent of works were competed only under rural connectivity and drought proofing types. Only 19 works of Rajiv Gandhi Seva Kendra was completed in Assam. In Assam, 51,964 numbers of works are running behind schedule, out of which 48,013 numbers of works are delayed by more than three months. 3,094 numbers of registered households in Assam are not even given job cards. Besides, 2,443 job card holders have not been paid the unemployment allowances.

Review of Earlier Studies

The main purpose of the review of literature pertaining to the evaluation of performances of NREGS in Assam is to give a proper orientation and perspective to the present work. A survey of literature places a significant role in establishing the backdrop for any research work in social sciences. It is felt that justification of present study can be made by reviewing the available literature on the subject. Therefore, an attempt has been made to review the literature on the subject so as to establish the relevance of the present study. There is extensive literature demonstrating the importance of NREGA in India's rural development. These studies can be mainly categorised in two different segments, *viz*; Potential of NREGA and Impact on rural households.

Since the launching of NREGA, there have been several studies looking into its implementation aspects, such as: wage formation processes in the rural labour markets, its finances, its democratic administration and implementation (Ambasta *et al.* 2008; Bardhan, 2011; Harrison, 2011; Khera *et al.* 2009; Shah, 2007). Some studies have focused on its socio-economic impact such as: rural poverty alleviation, gender issues, self-esteem, livelihood and food security and migration (Haberfeld *et al.* 2011; Sankaran, 2011; Tiwari *et al.* 2011; Zorlu *et al.* 2003; Raju, 2011; Rogaly, 2011). According to Ambasta *et al.* (2008), the reforms suggested in the Act can potentially transform the livelihoods of the poorest, heralding a revolution in rural governance in India. Many studies (Chakraborty, 2007; Raja, 2007; Mehrotra, 2008; Vijayakumar and Thomas, 2008; Hirway and Saluja, 2009) have examined empirically how various features of

NREGA, such as: access in rural areas, work guarantee, wage level and limited participation period, has influenced the welfare situation of the individual households. A lot of literature are found on NREGS in India wherein the details about the salient features of NREGA and its several relevant issues are articulated (*e.g.* Trivedi and Aswal, 2011 Thomas, 2008; Mahapatra, 2008; Patra and Dhal, 2009; Shamsi, 2007; Singh, 2008). A few studies of these further observed that the scheme is quite different from other employment scheme launched by the Government on many grounds.

There are also few studies which look at the implementation of NREGA in different states (Khera and Nayak, 2009; Dreze and Khera, 2009; Singh, 2009; Chhabra *et al.* 2009). Most of these studies showed that the coverage of NREGA at the micro level, *i.e.,* at the *panchayat* and village levels, has varied within the country. In other words, the Act has varied impact across states. Dreze and Khera (2009) observed that in some states, (*e.g.* Rajasthan and Himachal Pradesh) the Act has been very successful in terms of a large number of mandays of employment generated, works undertaken and payment of wages. On the other hand, in other states, the impact has been less remarkable (*e.g.* Bihar and Maharashtra). Some studies dealt with the performance of NREGA in some selected states of India which found satisfactory and some are not well versed (*e.g.* Trivedi and Aswal, 2011; Jacob and Varghese, 2006; Louis, 2006; Khera, 2008; Jeyaranjan, 2011; Jandu, 2008; Khera and Muthiah, 2010; Shrinivasan, 2012; Khera and Nayak, 2009). A lot of studies are also available which observed that NREGA is the successful scheme of the central Government to improve the condition of rural people (*e.g.* Puri, 2008; Bhatia and Dreze, 2006). Some specific studies are also available which explained the other segments of rural development issues in the context of NREGA (*e.g.* Das, 2007; Dreze, 2008). Singh and Mishra (2006) analysed the backward linkage or advance planning which is critical to the successful implementation of the Rural Employment Guarantee Scheme. Akthar and Azeez (2012) described that MGNREGA is an alternative avenue to arrest out-migration of unskilled, landless labourforce from the rural areas to urban areas by ensuing up to 100 days of wage employment within their native jurisdiction so that these guaranteed wage employment can be judiciously and rationally utilised by the landless peasants during lean and distress seasons. Krishnamurthy, 2006 analysed the NREGA and other related employment generation programmes from the perspective of responding to sudden (and rapid) onset of events like economic crises and natural and man-made disasters. Shah (2007) expressed that the NREGA has the potential to provide a 'big push' in India's region of distress. Patel (2006) in his work pointed out some important constraints of existing rural employment generation programmes and highlighted the Government's keenness to involve *Panchayati Raj* Institutions (PRIs) directly in NREGS. Saha Roy (2013) observed from different studies that there is continued illegal presence of contractors and delay in payments is a significant negative factor affecting the availability of work. In another study Goswami (2009) expressed that the Government of Andhra Pradesh has successfully implemented NREGA and the significant development regarding implementation of NREGA in the state of AP was that the use of Information Technology (IT) in all stages of implementation of NREGA work. Ambasta and Shah (2008) described the superiority of NREGA as a rural development scheme and further highlights the role of Information Technology (IT) in the effective application of NREGA. Siddhartha and Vanaik (2008) while dealing with the draft report of CAG (2007) on the working of NREGA, highlights some important constraints of implementation of NREGA and forwarded possible recommendation for the successful implementation of the scheme. Mehrotra (2008) examined the performance of NREGS since its inception and observed the key issues of design and implementation of the Scheme. Jacob and Varghese (2006) studied the implementation of NREGA in Kerala and the study reveals that the local bodies played a vital role in implementation of the Act. Louis (2006) analysed the poor performance of NREGA in Bihar and blamed the state government for its wrong implementation of what is holding back the Government of Bihar. Khera (2008) examines how the NREGA can empower the rural poor to demand a fair amount of employment at the minimum wage in Madhya Pradesh. Jeyaranjan (2011) examined the initial response to the NREGS in Tamil Nadu which are not satisfactory because of many reasons and further observed its subsequent reworking which is very encouraging. Jandu (2008) carried out a research in four states *viz*; Chhattisgarh, Madhya Pradesh, Orissa and Tamil Nadu and found that women workers are more confident about their roles as contributors to family expenditure and their work decisions and it gives them space in public sphere. The study also observed positive impact of the

MGNREGA on migration patterns. Khera and Muthiah (2010) have described that the scale of NREGA employment (average mandays per rural household) in Tamil Nadu which has increased steadily during first Phase. Further, there are significant achievements in the State in respect to women's participation and involvement of *Gram Panchayats* in the implementation of NREGA. Shrinivasan (2012) explained the 'success' of the MGNREGS in reducing the number of men migrating out of India's poorest states has become something truism. However, in Punjab the impact of NREGA on migrant labourers was not satisfactory. Khera and Nayak (2009) studied the progress of MGNREGA in six Hindi speaking states of North India focuses on impact of NREGA in the lives of women workers. This study reveals that there is significant benefits reported by women include increased food security and better ability to avoid hazardous work. Further, researchers (*e.g.* Ravindranath and Tiwari, 2009; Kumar, 2011; Tiwari and Somashekhar, 2011) studied the evaluation of NREGA and its effectiveness in well-being in Karnataka state. Ramesh and Kumar (2009) found that MGNREGA holds the powerful prospect of bringing major changes in the lives of women.

Many research works have done on wage system in MGNREGA scheme (*e.g.* Anindita and Bhatia, 2010; Vanaik and Siddarth, 2008; CAG, 2007; NCAER, 2009). MGNREGA has a demand driven Scheme so under this scheme part of funds 60 per cent expended on wages but due to irregularities in some cases work has been completed but wages have not been given to beneficiaries. Payments of wages through bank are another safe guard of this scheme but due to corruption and irregularities wage has been not received by beneficiaries. Employment and unemployment allowance have important part of MGNREGA scheme, this scheme given an assurance to rural people 100 days employment on nearer at home but unfortunately works were not provided within 15 days its provision under NREGA Act to provide unemployment allowance on this theme many research works have been done (*e.g.* Chandrashekhar and Ghosh, 2005; Dreze, Khera and Sidharth, 2006; Rai, 2010; Jha and Gaiha, 2012; Dutta, Murgai, Ravallion, Dominique van de Walle, 2012; Tiwari *et at.* 2011; Chowdhury, 2011; Hirway and Shah, 2011).

A lot of literature is also available on implementation of NREGA in North East India but have dearth of literature about the impact and performance of NREGA in Assam except a few wherein the poor performance and rampant abnormality in implementation are articulated (North East Social Trust Report, Indo-Global Social Service Society, other NGO report etc.). Borgohain (2005) highlighted that enactment of NREGA is a bold step addressed especially to the problem of galloping rural unemployment, commands a position of an unparallel significance in the eradication of unemployment in the rural areas. Hazarika (2009) examined the impact of MGNREGA on gender empowerment in Morigaon and Bongaigaon district of Assam. According to him majority of the respondents felt that they are now in better position to fulfill their own requirement without looking at others. He further observed that in Bongaigaon district, a large number of job card holders were found who have become *Panchayat* representatives. The study observed a lot of irregularities of the existing practices of NREGA. Goswami (2008) described that NREGA which have positive impact on the lives of millions of people across the poorest districts in the country. He observed that perhaps the most remarkable feature of NREGA is the programme which implemented without the agency of local contractors, who have emerged as major agents of exploitation of the rural poor. Panda, Dutta and Prusty (2009) found that NREGA empowered rural tribal women in Sikkim and Meghalaya by enhancing their confidence level and by ensuring some degree of financial independence. Panda and Umdor (2011) conducted a field study on the impact of MGNREGA in Assam and found that on an average only 42 per cent respondents remarked that MGNREGA had helped to uplift women. There has been no change in the status of women in four sample districts except Tinsukia. Bordoloi (2011) observed that the NREGA is a new lifeline of the rural people who earn their livelihood as wage earners. The scheme gears up the social relationship among the rural people which is a pre-requisite condition to build a strong society or a nation and also reduces the gender difference for some works which are in practice in rural areas. Ministry of Home Affairs, 2011[[2]] reported that MGNREGA has ushered in a new era of hope for the downtrodden states of Manipur and Nagaland. It is slowly and steadily transforming the 'Geography of Poverty'. Hazarika (2009) observed that the NREGA is a wage employment programme, providing minimum wage employment to casual, unskilled labour, especially during lean season. Its larger aim is to generate savings and assets in the countryside, to promote a growth process based on local development. The researcher found that the programme has indeed a positive impact on women empowerment, in so far as it has addressed a number of practical gender needs. Bhowmik (2013) put forward the argument that MGNREGS is of great importance in the state of Tripura. In terms of equity, the state appears to be doing pretty well, while from the point of efficiency, it is better than many states but there is scope of improvement.

Thus, there has been a spate of studies designed to assess the performance of MGNREGS ever since the Act relating to it came into being (Dreze and Khera, 2009; Mehrotra, 2008; Ambastha, Shankar and Shah, 2008; Gopal, 2009; Jha, Gaiha and Shankar, 2008; Jha, Bhattacharya, Gaiha, and Shankar, 2009; Jha, Gaiha and Shankar, 2009; Scandizzo, Gaiha and Imai, 2009). While some studies have drawn attention to huge leakage and fudging of muster rolls, others are not that critical and have been ecstatic over the number of jobs created, and number of beneficiaries from disadvantaged groups such as: the ST, SC and women etc. (Gaiha, Kulkarni, Pandey and Imai, 2009). This is symptomatic of the fact that while some studies have debunked this nation-wide programme, others are seen to endorse it on the grounds that it will transform the lives of poor and make them aware of their entitlement. In the light of this backdrop, this study attempts to investigate the implementation of MGNREGA in the state of Assam and North Eastern Region (henceforth NER) in general with emphasis on coverage of households, employment guaranteed, works undertaken, strengths, bottlenecks and strategies for further strengthening the programme. Moreover, the perceptions of the beneficiaries on functioning and the impact of the Scheme are also studied in this context.

Objectives

The main focus of the present study is to analyse the performance of MGNREGS in North East India in general and Assam in particular. More specifically the study is based on the following objectives.

(*a*) To review the functioning and performance of MGNREGS in Assam and North Eastern Region in particular.

(*b*) To examine the benefits, existing drawbacks and consequent impact of MGNREGA in the context of NER economy.

(*c*) To examine the perceptions of beneficiaries of MGNREGS on the function of MGNREGA in the study district.

(*d*) To suggest suitable measures for the effective implementation of the scheme.

Methodology

Since this research is basically evaluative in nature but little bit psychometrics approach is also resorted to get better understanding about the research problem. Both secondary and primary data sources were employed for the research. Primary data is collected through structured questionnaire distributed to the wages earners from the Nagaon districts of Assam from three development blocks (*viz*; Odali, Raha and Binakandi) from Nagaon district were selected under first level of random sampling. Again, from each development block five revenue villages were selected under second level of random sampling mostly those revenue villages which are featured with high proliferation of wage earners. Again from five revenue villages, twelve respondents from each are selected on third level of random sampling. In this way 180 respondents are selected of which 150 respondents questionnaire were found good and included in the study. The field data are collected during the month of February, 2013. Moreover, to get the reliable data from the respondents focus group method is also undertaken. Further, this study uses secondary data from various sources for assessing the performance of MGNREGS in NER of India and Assam in particular. Data relating MGNREGS are compiled from the secondary sources and the study period covers 2007-08 to 2012-13. Using official data this study evaluates India's National Rural Employment Guarantee Scheme according to criteria: *(a)* average number of days of employment per household; *(b)* percentage of households completing 100 days of employment under MGNREGS; *(c)* percentage of expenditure against total available funds etc. Further, comparative analysis is also made among Assam, North East India and India as a whole on the performance of MGNREGS.

Result and Analysis

Socio-economic Profile of the Respondents

The respondents of the study mainly belong to the age group of 35-45 yrs as 60.5 per cent of the respondents belong to that group. Out of total respondents 38 per cent are female. Further, study covers all sections of society wherein representation of Hindu (54%), Muslims (45%) and Christian (1%) are ensured. Moreover, out of 150 respondents 61 belong to general caste, 45 belong to SC community, 9 belong to ST and 35 belong to OBC and MOBC. Further, 67 per cent of the respondents have completed I-VII standard category of education level. Moreover, majority of the respondents are married and they live in nuclear family.

Performances of MGNREGS in India and North Eastern Region

NREGA later renamed as Mahatma Gandhi National Rural Employment Guarantee Act (MGNREGA) in 2009 passed with the objectives to provide work at remunerative wages to landless labourers and marginal farmers; and to create assets for raising agricultural productivity. The act became effective at the state level in February 2006 in 200 districts, guaranteeing employment up to 100 days a year to poor rural nouseholds on demand. Significantly, MGNREGA is a right-based programme, unlike earlier employment schemes. The rights of MGNREGA workers include employment on demand, minimum wages, gender parity of wages, and payment of wages within 15 days, as well as the provision of basic worksite facilities, among others. Further, 33 per cent participation in employment is reserved for women as laid down in the Act.

- *Women Participation:* There are many factors that encourage the women workers to participate in this scheme includes nature of work, limited hours of work, availability of work locally, reduction of migration of male member, substantial jump in the wage rate etc. Participation of women varies widely across the nation. At the national level participation of women has increased significantly from 46.41 per cent in 2010-11 to 48.81 per cent in 2011-12 and further to 53.01 per cent in 2012-13 (till January, 2013) which are exceeding expectations of stipulated 33 per cent share. Highest participation is seen in the state of Kerala (92.66%) followed by Poducherry (83.96%) in 2011-12. The share of women was less in states like: Bihar, Punjab, West Bengal and most of NER states. The participation rate of women in NER States is shown in Table 2.3.

From Table 2.3, it has come to light that none of the NER States of India could able to cross the national level of women participation in 2010-11 (46.41%) and 2011-12 (48.81%). Among the NER States of India, Tripura had the highest percentage in 2010-11 and Meghalaya in 2011-12 in case of women participation. Assam ranks the lowest category state in all the corresponding year just above to Mizoram. Table 2.4 depicts the participation of women and other sections in the total employment scenario under MGNREGS in 2012-13.

Table 2.3: Participation Rate of Women in North-Eastern States in India

States	Women Participation Rate (%)			
	2009-10	2010-11	2011-12	2012-13*
Assam	18.92	21.22	24.91	25
Manipur	30.34	29.87	33.58	36
Meghalaya	32.13	36.54	41.59	41
Mizoram	21.23	20.45	23.61	23
Nagaland	23.78	25.12	27.05	25
Tripura	36.67	37.67	38.64	41
Arunachal Pradesh	36.43	35.44	40.33	32
India	45.65	46.41	48.81	53

*upto Dec' 2012; Source: MGNREGA MIS Report of 2007 to 2012.

Table 2.4: Participation Rate of Women and Other Categories in NER, 2012-13*

States	Total (Mandays in Lakhs)	Women (Mandays in Lakhs)	% of Women Participation	Others (Mandays in Lakhs)	% of Other's Participation
Arunachal Pradesh	9.14	2.93	32.06	6.21	67.94
Assam	177.65	44.06	24.80	133.59	75.20
Manipur	89.87	32.32	35.96	57.55	64.04
Meghalaya	85.35	35.04	41.05	50.31	58.95
Mizoram	84.69	19.23	22.71	65.46	77.29
Nagaland	66.88	16.6	24.82	50.28	75.18
Sikkim	11.59	5.42	46.76	6.17	53.24
Tripura	340	140.89	41.44	199.11	58.56
India	14066.05	7473.85	53.13	6592.2	46.87

(*upto Dec. 2012); Source: Ministry of Rural Development, 2013.

Fig. 2.1 depicts that the share of women in Assam in MGNREGA which are in decreasing trend. At an average only 26.92 per cent women in Assam are employed under MGNREGA (MGNREGA MIS Report, 2012[[3]]) which is less than the earmark of 33 per cent as articulated in the Act.

The MGNREGA plays a significant role to meet the practical as well as strategic needs which are examined through the following parameters (Kar, 2013; Das, 2012):

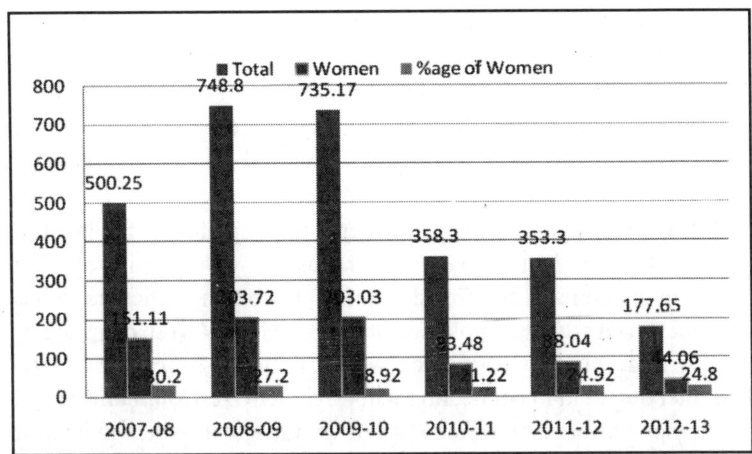

Fig. 2.1: **Women Employment Generated in Assam (Mandays in Lakhs)**

Source: MGNREGA MIS Report of 2007 to 2012.

(i) *Income-consumption effects:* An Income-consumption effect means an increase in income of women workers and consequent ability to choose their consumption baskets. In examining MGNREGA more emphasis is given to consumption because it is the main factor for judging income-consumption effects. If a woman earns but unable to spend for her own needs or surrender her income to the head of the household then the element of empowerment does not come. MGNREGA empowers women by giving them a scope of independent earning and spend some amount for their own needs.

(ii) *Intra-household effects:* Women play a major role in raising the economic resources for their family but their contribution remains uncounted because of their performance is not considered monetarily (unpaid work). In rural areas, the dominance of male in intra-household decisions has been seen. MGNREGA has significant impact in converting such unpaid work of women into paid work and widen the scope of decision making role of women in household matters. As the wages are paid through formal institutions, the intra-household status of women increases and they can control cash resources because withdrawn can be made only as per her own decision.

(iii) *Enhancement of choices and capability:* MGNREGA has widened the choice set for women by giving them independent income-earning opportunity. If a woman depends on the head of the household then her choice become the subject of household direction. It is reported that MGNREGA has enhanced the choice of women to use earnings.

(iv) *Community-level effects:* Women's participation at the local or district level of governance process is low in spite of 73rd Amendments of the Constitution. But women participation has increased after the implementation of MGNREGA in many areas. A large number of women workers attended the *gram-sabha* meeting held in connection with MGNREGA. Community level empowerment of women is one of the great achievements of this Act.

- *Physical and Financial Achievements of MGNREGS:* The MGNREGS is an unparalleled rural reconstruction programme to transform the Indian rural economic scene. It has already been stated that the MGNREGS is a unique weapon in the economic history of independent India to remove rural poverty and unemployment. It is a revolutionary step for India's poor. This would not only help the eradication of rural unemployment but would put a check on migration of rural people to the urban areas. In this section an attempt has been made to examine the performance of MGNREGS in Assam and North East India.

Assam, one of the major states of NER is also covered under MGNREGS. In Assam, the five tribal dominated districts *i.e.,* Karbi Anglong, Kokrajhar, Dima Hasao, Lakhimpur and Dhemaji were the beneficiary district of MGNREGS in the first phase of implementation of the Scheme in 2006-07. The Scheme was extended to Barpata, Bongaigaon, Cachar, Darrang, Goalpara, Hailakandi, Morigaon and Nalbari districts in 2007-08 and from 1st April, 2008 the Scheme was implemented in all the remaining districts of Assam. It is observed that since the inception of MGNREGS in Assam, there has been a welcome and widespread social acceptance of the scheme and has received an overwhelming response from the people living in the rural areas. This section basically deals with detail analysis of performance of the MGNREGS in Assam during 2007-08 to 2012-13. The performance of MGNREGS in Assam during 2007-08 to 2012-13 has been presented in terms of physical achievements, financial performance, job card issues and employment generated under MGNREGS.

Table 2.5 presents the achievements of MGNREGS in Assam during 2007-08 to 2011-12. It is apparent from the table that during reference period, the MGNREGS was able to generate 2,695.82 lakh mandays of employment of which 24.91 per cent to women. The employment generated to SC and ST was 9.62 per cent and 30.06 per cent respectively while 60.32 per cent of the total employment belonged to the other communities. Thus, the lion's share of the employment was occupied by the other communities including OBC and MOBC etc.

Table 2.5: Physical Achievements under MGNREGS in Assam, 2007-08 to 2011-12 (Figures within Brackets Indicate Percentage)

Year	Employment Generated (Mandays in Lakhs)			
	SC	ST	Others	Total
2007-08	40.69 (8.13)	191.37 (38.26)	268.19 (53.61)	500.25
2008-09	78.08 (10.42)	258.32 (34.50)	412.40 (55.08)	748.80
2009-10	89.03 (12.11)	227.36 (30.92)	418.78 (56.97)	735.17
2010-11	19.78 (5.53)	69.94 (19.51)	268.58 (74.96)	358.30
2011-12	31.72 (8.99)	63.28 (17.91)	258.30 (73.11)	353.3
Total	259.3 (9.62)	810.27 (30.06)	1626.25 (60.32)	2695.82

Source: Statistical Hand Book, Assam 2007; 2008; 2009; 2010 and 2011

Table 2.6 shows the physical achievements in terms of employment and participation of different segments of beneficiaries under MGNREGS in NER, 2012-13. It is observed that most of the tribal populations of the NER of India are benefited from MGNREGS except Assam.

If we look at the break up of financial performance of MGNREGS funds in NER, it is observed that Tripura is the highest recipient of MGNREGS fund followed by Assam (Table 2.10). The Administrative expenditure is very high in Sikkim resulting very low percentage of expenditure on wages. As a whole in India expenditure against total available fund is 63.29 per cent, out of which 76.38 per cent utilised on expenditure on wages, 23.62 per cent utilised on expenditure on material, and 4.61 per cent utilised on administrative heads.

Table 2.6: Physical Achievements under MGNREGS in Assam, 2012-13

States	Employment Generated (Mandays in Lakhs)						
	Total	SCs	%of SC	STs	%of ST	Others	%of other's
Arunachal Pradesh	9.14	0.00	0.02	7.94	86.85	1.2	13.13
Assam	177.65	10.08	5.68	34.15	19.22	133.42	75.10
Manipur	89.87	0.83	0.93	52.10	57.97	36.94	41.10
Meghalaya	85.35	0.46	0.54	80.67	94.51	4.22	4.94
Mizoram	84.69	0.01	0.01	84.47	99.74	0.21	0.25
Nagaland	66.88	0.02	0.03	62.75	93.82	4.11	6.15
Sikkim	11.59	0.53	4.55	3.59	30.97	7.47	64.45
Tripura	340.00	59.30	17.44	145.26	42.72	135.44	39.84
India	14066.05	3142.07	22.34	2214.22	15.74	8709.76	61.92

Source: Ministry of Rural Development, 2013.

The financial performances of MGNREGS in Assam during 2007-08 to 2011-12 are shown in the Fig. 2.2. It is evident from the Fig. 2.2 that during 2007-08 to 2011-12, the total expenditure incurred under MGNREGS in Assam was 3,83,774.72 lakh as against 4,67,992.96 lakh available funds. The percentage of expenditure was 82 per cent during the study period. It is pertinent to note that during 2010-11, the expenditure was much higher (165.48%) than the total fund released under the Scheme while the percentage of expenditure is too low in 2007-08.

Table 2.8 represents the Job card issued and employment provided under MGNREGS in Assam during the period 2007-08 to 2011-12. It is evident from the Table 2.8 that during the period MGNREGS could provide employment to 8091602 rural households as against 15863365 Job cards. Fig. 2.3 depicts the job card issued and employment provided under MGNREGA in different years in Assam. It shows that during 2007-08 to 2010-11, the Scheme was able to generate employment to only 51.01 per cent of the total Job card holders which means half of the job card holders do not get the required number of guaranteed job which was more acute in the initial years.

Table 2.7: Financial Performances under MGNREGS in NER in 2012-13*

States	Total Funds Available (in Crore)	Total Expd. (in Crore)	% of Expd. against Total Available Fund	% of Expd. on Wages	% of Expd. on Material	% of Adm. Expd.
Arunachal Pradesh	40.09	11.00	27.43	91.04	8.96	2.53
Assam	509.56	389.49	76.44	65.99	34.01	5.18
Manipur	478.25	160.66	33.59	81.08	18.92	1.53
Meghalaya	205.74	158.58	77.08	71.64	28.36	3.75
Mizoram	267.25	142.68	53.39	85.33	14.67	5.21
Nagaland	255.51	123.57	48.36	67.07	32.93	0.00
Sikkim	60.86	27.41	45.05	61.43	38.57	6.13
Tripura	1355.65	559.52	41.27	76.67	23.33	3.40
India	39620.16	25074.69	63.29	76.38	23.62	4.61

(*upto December, 2012); Source: Ministry of Rural Development, 2013

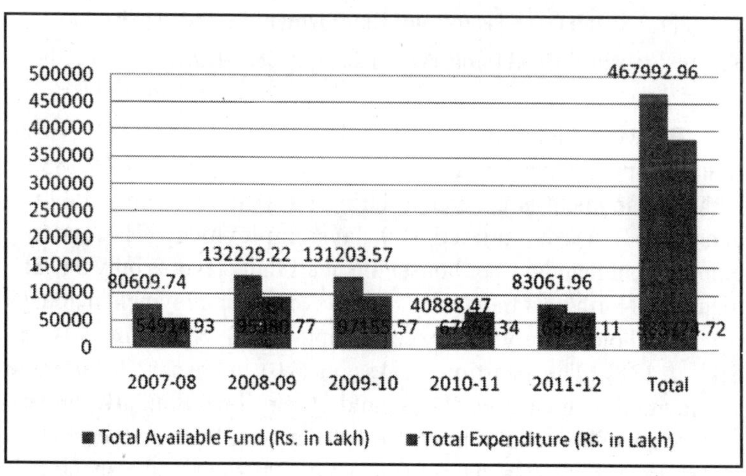

Fig. 2.2: **Financial Performance under MGNREGA in Assam**

Source: Statistical Hand Book, Assam 2007; 2008; 2009; 2010 and 2011

Table 2.8: Job Card Issued and Employment Provided in Assam, 2007-08 to 2011-12

Year	Total No. of Job Cards Issued	No. of Households Provided Employment	Percentage
Total	15863365	8091602	51.01

Source: Statistical Hand Book, Assam 2007; 2008; 2009; 2010 and 2011

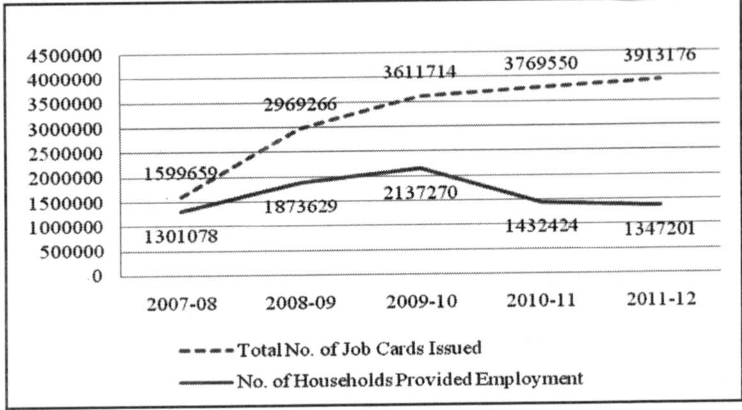

Fig. 2.3: **Job Card Issued and Employment Provided in Assam**

Source: Statistical Hand Book, Assam 2007; 2008; 2009; 2010 and 2011

Table 2.9 depicts the operational performance of MGNREGS in India during financial year 2012-13. It is observed that 16,183.61 lakhs employment is generated during the year while only 3.29 per cent of HH has completed 100 days employment. The average employment mandays per household at all India level is only 34. The picture of North East India in respect to average employment mandays per household is very bad except Tripura (58), Mizoram (49) and Sikkim (38). The position of Assam (20) in respect to average employment mandays per household is very low. Similarly in case percentage of households provided 100 days employment the position of Assam is very low and this is just above Mizoram and Nagaland. It is observed that the picture of percentage of households provided 100 days employment; the position Sikkim and Tripura is near about the all India average.

Table 2.9: Operational Performance of MGNREGS in NER in 2012-13 (Employment Generated, Mandays in Lakhs)

States	Total	Average Mandays Per Household	No. of Households Availed 100 days Employment	% of HH Completed 100 days Employment
Arunachal Pradesh	4.13	20	913	2.02
Assam	177.47	20	1201	0.13
Manipur	69.26	27	58	0.02
Meghalaya	39.27	34	9954	3.96
Mizoram	19.44	49	0	0.00
Nagaland	20.72	29	0	0.00
Sikkim	12.89	38	1149	3.75
Tripura	276.32	58	17897	3.07
India	16183.61	34	1365649	3.29

Source: Ministry of Rural Development, 2013.

Fig. 2.4 depicts the data on 100 days of employment provided under MGNREGS in Assam during 2007-08 to 2011-12. It reveals that during the reference period, the total 80, 91,602 rural households provided employment under MGNREGS. Out of 80, 91,602 households, only 5, 86,304 households (7.25%) provided 100 days employment opportunities under the Scheme.

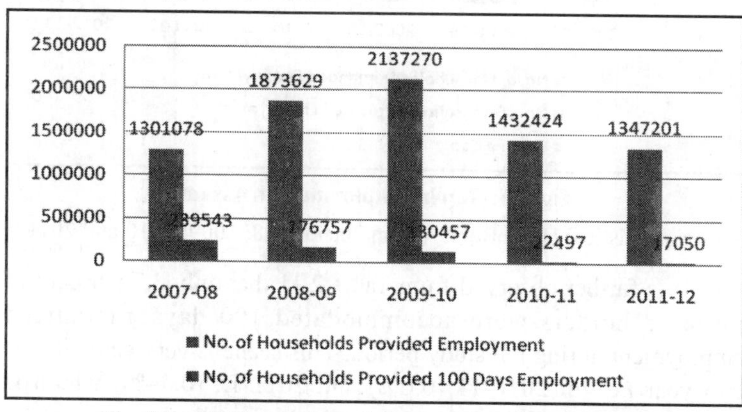

Fig. 2.4: **100 Days of Employment Provided in Assam**

Source: Compiled the data from Statistical Hand Book, Assam

Table 2.10 depicts the total gap during the period of study in the existing demand and supply of employment avenues in MGNREGS in Assam in different years. The success of the movement can better be explained that the scheme is sufficient enough to provide employment to all unemployed masses of the state which is evident from the number of households demanded employment and No. of Households provided employment. Further, from Fig. 2.5, it is observed that sincere effort of the government has resulted the decreasing trend during the years under study.

Table 2.10: Gap in Employment in Assam, 2007-08 to 2011-12

Year	No. of Households Demanded Employment	No. of Households Provided Employment	Existing Gap	Percentage of Gap
Total	8441735	8091602	350133	4.15

Source: Statistical Hand Book Assam 2007; 2008; 2009; 2010 and 2011.

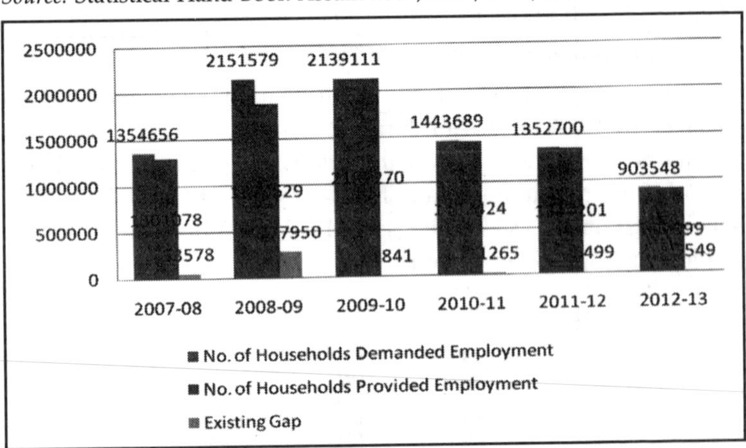

Fig. 2.5: **Gap in Employment in Assam**

Source: Statistical Hand Book Assam 2007; 2008; 2009; 2010 and 2011

It is further observed from Table 2.11 that only 3.7 per cent of job card holders were accommodated 100 days guaranteed employment during the study period. This scene is very acute in last two year *i.e.,* in 2010-11 (0.6%) and 2011-12 (0.44%) which is observed from the Fig. 2.6.

Table 2.11: 100 Days of Employment Provided in Assam, 2007-08 to 2011-12

Year	Total No. of Job Cards Issued	No. of Households Provided 100 Days Employment	P/C
Total	15863365	586304	3.70

Source: Statistical Hand Book Assam 2007; 2008; 2009; 2010 and 2011

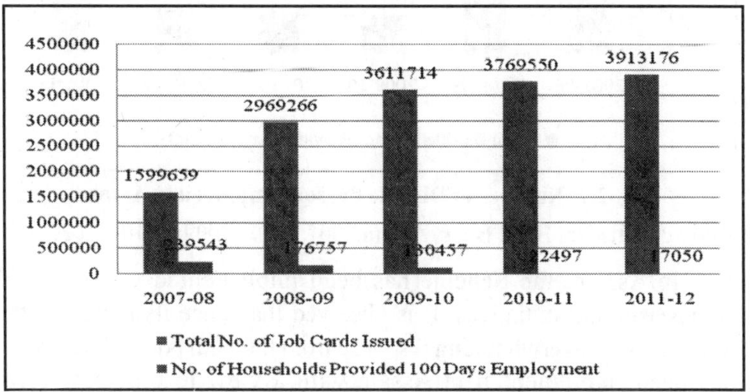

Fig. 2.6:**100 Days of Employment Provided in Assam;**

Source: Statistical Hand Book, Assam 2007; 2008; 2009; 2010 and 2011

Fig. 2.7 depicts the number of disable person employed in Assam provided employment in different years. During the study period a total of 12,274 disable persons were provided employment. As per the Persons with Disability Act (PWD) of 1995, NREGA should provide 3 per cent employment to the disabled. However, Assam provided 0.036 per cent employments only to the disabled in the last year.

Thus, it appears from the above that though the MGNREGS is the bold and most pragmatic approach to the problems of rural poverty and unemployment but the success of the scheme in Assam is very poor. In fact, the Scheme fails to ensure the economic security of the rural poor by providing guaranteed wage employment in Assam. Though the Scheme is an important milestone in the eradication of rural poverty and unemployment problem in India which has added a new dimension to the unemployment problem of the country but the success of the movement still remains questionable. The Government of India though has kept high hopes on MGNREGS to achieve its noble objectives but needs more steps for its successful implementation.

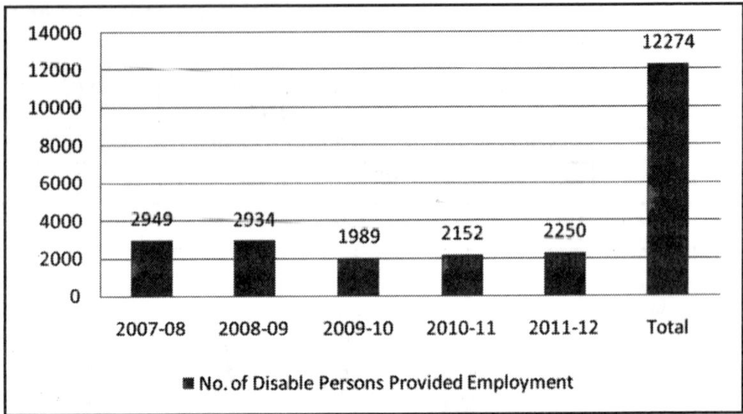

Fig. 2.7: **Number of Disable Person Employed in Assam**

Source: Statistical Hand Book, Assam 2007; 2008; 2009; 2010 and 2011.

In Assam, the Scheme has been implemented with a lot of enthusiasm and initiatives. It is observed that since its inception the State receives overwhelming response from the rural poor. The Scheme has been implemented in Assam with a view to eradicate rural unemployment. During 2007-08 to 2011-12, the Government of Assam has spent Rupees 3, 83,774.72 lakh under MGNREGS to generate 5,863.04 lakh mandays of employment. It is pertinent to note that during the reference period MGNREGS could provide employment to 8,091,602 rural households out of which 586304 households *i.e.* 7.25 per cent of the total households have been provided 100 days of wage employment. This clearly indicates the poor performance of the scheme in Assam. MGNREGA in North Eastern Region of India in general and Assam in particular not provided 100 days security to workers. Further, during the period 2006-07- 2012-13, MGNREGA created social inclusion and given approximately 33.7 per cent jobs for women's which is just higher from secure in MGNREGA Act.

Benefits of MGNREGS toward National Economy

Workfare programmes not only typically provide unskilled workers with short-term employment on public works but also income transfers to poor households during periods when they suffer on account of absence of opportunities of employment. In areas with high unemployment rates and under employment, transfer benefits from workfare programmes can prevent poverty from worsening, especially during lean periods. As requisite infrastructure is created, the durable assets created by these programmes have the potential to generate second round employment benefits. In broader sense, the MGNREGA will help the government in: *(a)* overcoming growing stockpiles of food grains; *(b)* ensuring water security and market connectivity; *(c)* preventing rural-urban migration and *(d)* development of human capital.

Since the Government of India holds food grains far in excess of the quantity required to achieve food security, the MGNREGA offers the Government the opportunity to use this excess of grains to finance labour for the development of rural infrastructure. Utilisation of excess grains to finance the scheme will serve two purposes: *(i)* paying a part of the wages in term of grain will avoid the inflationary tendency in other wage goods that may arise due a sudden transfer of purchasing power and *(ii)* it will reduce the outlay on food subsidy by significantly reducing the carrying cost of grain. The MGNREGA will provide the Government with a means to reduce expenditure on the current account and improve the fiscal health of the Government.

The rural India is facing an increasing problem of water security due to lack of irrigation infrastructure. Water levels all over the country have been falling due to over-exploitation of ground water resources. It is believed that the MGNREGA offers a 'historic opportunity' to address this problem (Shah, 2007). The expenditure on public works under the MGNREGA can be directed towards construction of irrigation apparatus, which would alleviate the problem of water security to some extent. The funds allocated under the MGNREGA are also used for development of roads thereby connecting villages to national highways and thus facilitating connectivity with markets.

The MGNREGA will have significant positive impact on seasonal rural-urban migrations by providing employment to rural workers during the lean season (Khandelwal and Chawla, 2006). This will reduce the problem of excessive population pressures in Indian cities as surplus rural labour will find employment in their own districts. The MGNREGA may also have an impact on permanent migrations trends (Shah, 2012).

Though it is difficult to ascertain the impact, one can assume that the created infrastructure and the increased activity in the rural economy due to increased purchasing power will lead to higher rates of permanent job creation, thereby mitigating the urgency to migrate.

Further, the public works have the potential to develop human capital by promoting skills in rural India. This may be through 'learning-by-doing' kind of processes or through formal training of the workers by trained personnel (Khandelwal and Chawla, 2006). This shall reduce the dependence of the rural population on agriculture by enabling them to move on to other activities. Thus, MGNREGA has several potential benefits of reviving the economy as it is self targeting, self adjusting and self liquidating.

Beneficiaries Perception on Potential Benefits of MNREGA

The implementation of MNREGA is likely to bring many changes in various aspects such as: level of food security, migration situation, indebtedness, poverty level, economic independence of women etc. for the rural community. For assessing the direction and magnitude of changes, beneficiaries were asked to give their opinions on changes they observed owing to implementation of MNREGA. The results based on these perceptions are presented in Table 2.12.

Table 2.12: Beneficiaries Perception on Potential Benefits of MNREGA

Potential Benefits	No. of House Holds (Figure in Parenthesis Represent Percentage)				
	To Some Extent	Some Extent	Large Extent	No	Not Sure
Enhancing food security	36 (24%)	21 (14%)	13 (8.67%)	54 (36%)	26 (17.33%)
Protect extreme poverty	54 (36%)	18 (12%)	3 (2%)	52 (34.67%)	23 (15.33%)
Reduce distress migration	51 (34%)	11 (7.33%)	0 (0%)	52 (34.67%)	36 (24%)
Reduce indebtedness	28 (18.67%)	19 (12.67%)	0 (0%)	60 (40%)	43 (28.67%)
Greater economic independence to women	76 (50.67%)	30 (20%)	0 (0%)	24 (16%)	20 (13.33%)
Improves socio-economic conditions	48 (32%)	18 (12%)	5 (3.33%)	54 (36%)	25 (16.67%)

Source: Field Survey.

From Table 2.12, it is evident that on the whole 46.67 per cent sample beneficiaries reported improvement in food security. About 36 households (24%) reported marginal improvement whereas remaining 34 households (22.67%) reported somewhat/large extent of improvement in food security. Only 36 per cent of the respondents denied the statement while 17.33 per cent could not make any comment about the statement. Thus, as per participants, MNREGA caused improvement in food availability for number of beneficiary households.

As regards to protection against extreme poverty, 50 per cent (75 HHs.) expressed that MNREGA provided protection against extreme poverty. Incremental income earned through MNREGA saved them from worsening their poverty due to very high rate of inflation. In majority cases, protection against extreme poverty was marginal. In respect of reducing extent of distress migration, overall 62 households (41.33%) believed that MNREGA helped in reducing the incidences of distress migration.

As regards to reduction in indebtedness, 47 households (31.34%) indicated that MNREGA helped in marginal to moderate reduction in the indebtedness, while 40 per cent of the respondents claimed that the MGNREGA could not benefited in reducing indebtedness at all.

Further, one of the goals of MNREGA is to give greater economic independence to women. In this context 80.67 per cent (106 HHs.) reported that owing to MNREGA, economic independence of women increased. However, in majority cases, increase in economic independence of women was marginal (50.67%). As regards improvement if socio-economic sphere of life by MGNREGA, majority of respondent 47.33 per cent of respondents claimed positive impact while only 36 per cent of respondents reported 'no improvement' on this issue. Thus, results suggests that implementation of MNREGA enhanced food security, reduced indebtedness and distress migration and enhanced economic vis-a-vis social independence of women of rural households. However, improvement in food security and other aspects varied from marginal to moderate.

Impact of MGNREGA

Any Act has three types of impact on the society-short term, medium term and the long-term. It may also affect a given society at three levels-the value system, the institutions, and the processes. MGNREGA is one of the most recent Acts of India in the context of rural development. Unfortunately there are very limited empirical evidences to present any observation regarding the medium term and long term effects of the Act. Further, there is insufficient basis to discuss the nature of impact of this Act upon the values or institutions. But there are enough studies to help us in finding out the short-term as well as the procession aspects of the impact of the Scheme by the Indian State in the context of empowerment of the rural poor particularly the most vulnerable sections like women, SCs and STs.

A panel survey conducted by the National Sample Survey Organization (NSSO) on the MGNREGA in 3 states shows that the Scheme provides work at a time when no other work or alternate employment opportunities exist. The Scheme has also contributed to ensuring greater food security, monthly per capita expenditure, savings etc., (Ministry of Rural Development, 2013[[4]]). A recent report by a global research organization indicates that for the first time in nearly 25 years, growth in rural spending outpaced urban consumption in the two years between 2009-10 and 2011-12. It also concluded that the increase in rural consumption is driven in significant part by the MGNREGA (CRISIL Research Insight, 2012[[5]]). To ascertain the impact of MGNREGs on different fields, the following points are incorporated.

- *Financial Inclusion:* To ensure transparency in wage payments and prevent misappropriations, the Government of India mandated that all MGNREGA wage payments should be made through banks/ post office accounts opened in the name of the worker. As a result, In India nearly 8.6 crore bank/post office accounts (4.08 crore accounts in Banks and 4.53 crore in Post Offices) of rural people have been opened under MGNREGA and around 80 per cent of MGNREGA payments are made through this route. The opening of accounts has brought the poor into the organized sector and in some cases provided them with better access to credit, an unprecedented financial inclusion initiative.
- *Inclusive Growth:* The Scheme also provides an alternative source of income for rural labourers, raising the reservation wage and implicitly offering labourers bargaining powers in an otherwise inequitable rural labour market. The Scheme has provided labourers (particularly those who are in debt bondage or contract labour) with a dignified choice of work (MGNREGA Sameeksha, 2013[[6]]). MGNREGA has also reduced distress migration from traditionally migration-intensive areas.

- *Women's Empowerment:* Various provisions under the Act aims to ensure that women have equitable and easy access to work, decent working conditions, equal payment of wages and representation on decision-making bodies. From 2006-07 up to 2012-13 (up to Dec., 2012), around Rupees 62,000 crore have been spent on wages for women. Women participation rate in India has ranged in between 40 per cent to 48 per cent of the total mandays generated much above the statutory minimum requirement of 33 per cent in India but the rate of such participation NER of India is very low.

In fact, the participation rate of women under the Scheme has been higher than in all forms of recorded work. Research studies indicate that MGNREGA is an important work opportunity for women who would have otherwise remained unemployed or underemployed (MGNREGA Sameeksha, 2013 [7]). With an increased rate of participation and large amounts being spent on wages for women, various studies suggest a positive impact of the Scheme on the economic well-being of women. The Scheme has also led to gender parity in wages. The NSSO 66th Round indicated that MGNREGA has reduced traditional wage discrimination in public works. Access to economic resources has also had a favourable impact on the social status of women. A large percentage of these women spend their money to avoid hunger, repay small debts, paying their child's schooling etc.

- *Impact on Agricultural Productivity:* Provision of water is vital for agriculture and ensuring food and water security in rural India. Research suggests that water-related assets created under MGNREGA have increased the number of days in a year water is available and also the quantity of water available for irrigation. The increased availability of water has also led to changes in cropping patterns and increased area under cultivation according to some studies.
- *Other Impact:* NREGA has made a dent on poverty by increasing employment opportunities in India. During the first year of implementation (2006-07) in 200 districts, 2.10 crore households were employed and 90.5 crore mandays were generated in India. In 2007-08, 3.39 crore households were provided employment and 143.59 crore mandays were generated in 330 districts of India. In 2008-09, 4.51 crore households have been provided employment and 216.32 crore mandays have been generated across the country.

A survey by the North East Social Trust and a few other voluntary organizations of Assam monitoring the impact of this Act and implementation during last couple of years has found the result very disappointing. For the financial year 2011-12 NEST carried out an intensive research on the basis of the Governments data to find out the implications of the Act in the state. It was reported that during the whole year (2011-12) Assam could provide 100 days employment to only 1.04 per cent job card holders. Further, the status of implementation of India's flagship rural job guarantee scheme MGNREGA was very poor in Assam during 2010-11. More than 24 lakh households (65% of the total registered MGNREGA card holders in the state) did not get job in the entire 2010-11 under MGNREGA. In Assam only 16,473 households got job for 100 days in the year and 611,032 households got job for less than 15 days as reported by NEST Report 2013.

North East Social Trust is working in NER for strengthening of rural livelihood opportunities and local governance in the region. In collaboration with Centre for Microfinance and Livelihood, NEST carried out the research to understand the rural livelihood status under MGNREGA in the state of Assam on completion of financial year 2010-11. Highlights of the findings on MGNREGA implementation in Assam in 2010-11 depict very abysmal implementation (NEST Report, 2013[[8]]). Total number of households that got job card in Assam is 3,749,672. Out of this the number of BPL families registered in MGNREGA is 25,616 which is 0.67 per cent of total registered household. District with highest percentage of BPL inclusion in MGNREGA is Dhubri with 1.53 per cent. This figure implies a very poor implementation. It is also found that the total 6 per cent of the job card holders belong to SC, 16 per cent ST and 78 per cent belongs to other categories. Further, a total of 24, 36,848 households (65%) did not get job in the entire year under MGNREGA in the year 2010. While only 16,473 numbers of house hold got 100 days employment in the year which is 0.56 per cent of the total Job card holding household. 611,032 numbers of household got less than 15 days employment in the year which is 21 per cent of the total Job card holding HHs. What is more worrisome is that 28,635 numbers of registered families are not given job card in the year and 29,331 mandays of unemployment allowances are not paid in the state during the period. Percentage of workers having bank account numbers is 41.13 per cent. Work execution level analysis for the Year 2010-2011 shows that 42.9 per cent of the work is being executed through GPs violating the norm of minimum 50 per cent execution through the GPs. Further, the total number of households which got job cards in 2012-13 in all the 27 districts of the State is 39, 49,587. Of these, only 12, 10,427 households got work in the last fiscal year. Among these 9,788 job card holding households got 100 days of work; 3,21,391 households got less than 10 days work and 6,90,965 households got at least 15 days work. The performance of Karimganj and Dima Hasao districts is poor with none of the households with jobs cards getting 100 days work (Union Ministry for Rural Development, 2013[[9]]).

Major Drawbacks

A good number of poverty alleviation schemes have been put in rural part of India since independence MGNREGA one of them but important thing is that it's provided 100 days legal jobs guarantee in rural part of India for who is willing to do unskilled manual work under this scheme. Since inception, NER of India faces many irregularities in implementation of this scheme like irregularities in Job card distribution, delay in wage payment, poor selection of work projects, non-preparation of Muster roll etc. Unawareness about this scheme is another bigger issue under this Scheme because many rural peoples who are necessary want to do jobs nearer to living place was not aware from this scheme

(a) *Awareness generation and information education communication:* The MGNREGA has the potential to provide a 'big push' in India's region of distress as claimed by various researchers. For MGNREGA to be able to realise its potential, the role of civil society nations is critical. But this calls for a new self-critical politics of fortitude, balance and restraint as reported by Shah (2007). Except a few awareness generation workshops and training of PRI functionaries, there are no regular sustained awareness programmes for the scheme for the benefit of district officials and villagers. It is observed that most of the officials at the field level do not have an overview of their project and MGNREGA programme and usually carry out the schemes according to the orders from above only. Moreover, in many states in India women participation is low because of low level of awareness about the process and entitlements of the programme.

Many of the male folks have withdrawn from agricultural activities and joined works in MGNREGA. This vacated space in agriculture has been occupied by the womenfolk and this scene is observed mostly in NER of India (Panda and Umdor, 2011). Further, it was witnessed that there is lack of awareness among the villagers, especially among the people who live in the interior villages of the *panchayat*. Hence, building awareness is a must to avoid deficiency in understanding the importance of MGNREGA amongst villagers.

(b) *Transparency and accountability:* Transparency and accountability are sins qua non to MGNREGS are in built in every project. As per the guidelines of the Act District Project Co-ordinator will be responsible to ensure transparency and accountability under the scheme (Singh, 2008). For ensuring transparency, some steps like display of the list of works and persons employed on the *Panchayats* notice board and prominent places are also undertaken but still transparency remains within red tape.

(c) *Work process, planning, projects and execution:* It is reported in many studies that no consolidated list is prepared and most officials have no idea about the nature and volume of project undertaken in the district. Further, there is hardly any integration of projects taken up in various adjacent blocks because of lack of co-ordination among project co-ordinators. As a whole there is no overall district development plan leading to ad-hoc block wise shelf of projects with little integration coordination and convergence.

(d) *Nature of work*: Most of the studies reveal that nature of work is also not helpful for women workers. Most of the projects selected being related to rural connectivity and renovation of local water bodies involving earth work requiring application of physical force, male workers were preferred to women workers (Hazarika, 2009).

(e) *Wage payment:* It is reported in many studies that there are frequent complaints that the present wage rate which is below market rate and also about delays in making wage payment. Another issue raises by Sankaran (2011) about the feasibility of having a national minimum wage, the NREGA with its provision for a country-wide wage rate has placed the possibility to do so squarely on the agenda. The MGNREGA wage rate must logically

be a need-based national minimum wage under the Minimum Wages Act. Vanaik and Siddhartha (2008) have explained that the payment of wages into bank accounts for work carried out under the MGNREGA has been suggested as a way to prevent embezzlement of funds. Union Minister of Rural Development Jairam Ramesh has taken a decision favouring payment of minimum wages for agricultural workers and the wages should not be lower than the minimum wages. The wages would be revised annually and a full revision would be effected every five years in consultation with the States.

(f) *Records:* It is often reported that there is a lack of systematic maintenance of records at block level. The shortage of IT skilled staff, interruption in power supply and non-availability of technical staffs etc. are some of the common problems.

(g) *Staff training and administrative set up:* In general, there is shortage of field staff and proposal for sanction of staff are pending for approval of the state government. CAG Report (2007)[[10]] has singled out lack of dedicated administrative and technical staff for MGNREGA as the key constraint responsible for procedural lapses.

(h) *Monitoring:* The MGNREGA evolves a strict monitoring-cum-concurrent evaluation mechanism for successful implementation of MGNREGS in the country. The Act provides a variety of monitoring activities at the various levels of implementation i.e. from village to central level. However, it is reported in many studies that there seems to be no detailed guidelines and standard operating audit procedures except at the central level.

(i) *Non-availability of child care facilities*: One of the major shortcomings of the Act is non-availability of child care and raring facilities at the worksite even though the Act includes this provision. Various studies shows that women remained worried about their children while they are working at MGNREGA worksite even some women do not accept the job facilities of MGNREGA because of non-availability of proper child care facilities.

(j) *Poor worksite facilities*: MGNREGA funds have been allocated for the provision of safe drinking water, resting place, changing

room, first aid, recreational facility for children etc. But most of the studies reported that except drinking water facility all other facilities were generally absent.

(k) *Illegal presence of contractors*: The continued illegal presence of contractors is a significant negative factor affecting the availability of work by women (Khera and Nayak, 2009).

(l) *Social audit:* A social audit is an ongoing process through which the potential beneficiaries and other stakeholders of an activity or project are involved at every stage – from planning to implementation, monitoring and evaluation. This process helps in ensuring that the activity or project is designed and implemented in a that most suited to the prevailing conditions, appropriately reflects the priorities and preferences of those affected by it, and most effectively serve public interest [[11]]. To ensure transparency and accountability, social auditing and inspection of MGNREGA work for proper assessment along with measuring of appropriateness, some steps are to be taken as per the Act of MGNREGA [[12]]. But the success of social audit still remains questionable (Gopal, 2009). The social audit process has a long way to go before it can claim to have contributed to transparency, empowerment and good governance. Further, it is observed from the survey of literature (NEST Report) that in 2010-11, 18 districts *viz*; Bongaigaon, Karbi Anglong, Kokrajhar, Lakhimpur, Borpeta, Cachar, Darrang, Hilakandi, Nalbari, Dhubri, Dibrugarh, Kamrup Rural, Kamrup Metro, Nagaon, Sivasagar, Sonitpur, Tinsukia and Udalguri showed 100 per cent social audit and no record of verification was found in 4 districts *viz*; Goalpara, Golaghat, Jorhat, and Karimganj. The lowest 32.14 per cent found in North Cachar Hills. It appears that there is no established procedure and system for undertaking social audit.

(m) *Lack of systematic work schedule:* A proper and more systematic work calendar is needed at the *Gram Panchayat* level for planning works mainly in the agricultural lean seasons. In the absence of this calendar, the ability of the programme to strengthen the agricultural sector is adversely affected. Labour shortages in agricultural sector have also been aggravated due to MGNREGA works.

(n) *Fool-proof system in case of funding:* During the course of interviews of the beneficiary households, some of them had expressed concern about the role of middlemen in case of fund disbursement for different projects. According to them, some middlemen were involved in illegal nexuses with corrupt government officials, siphoning away the funds provided for implementation of projects. Such corruption would hamper the effectiveness of MGNREGA. The only way corruption can be stemmed is by proactive people's involvement in the implementation process. People should actively question the officials for transparency in the process and get proper information about creation of muster rolls and disbursement of funds.

(o) *Discrepancies and favouritism:* Some villagers reported discrepancies and favoritism for the number of days of employment. Again, few villagers have also alleged that there is a tendency of local influential people of the village to get their names registered in the muster roll, without actually engaging themselves in the assigned projects. This leads to work burden on the other labourers as their work is divided amongst the workers in order to provide wages to them. This is a serious issue and it should be checked immediately by bringing it under the purview of the PO/ Block level officers.

Perceptions of Beneficiaries on Functioning of MGNREGA

Here attempt has been made to assess the functioning of MGNREGA based on the perception of participations on various aspects. The qualitative questions related with awareness on various aspects of MGNREGA, quality of assets created, issuance of job card, difficulties faced, suggestions to improve functioning of MGNRGA etc., have been asked to sample beneficiaries.

- *About Job Card:* As per guideline, issue of job-card to applicant household is done by *Gram Panchayat*. The job card validity is of 5 years. Also there is a provision to issue job card with photograph free of cost. There is no application fee for issuance of job card. 68 per cent households reported that getting job card from the authority is not simple though 93.33 per cent respondents said that they had not paid any fees or bribes for getting job-card. However, 6.67 per cent sample beneficiary houscholds reported that they had to pay some amount as fees or bribes for getting job card. Further, 88 per cent respondents reported that they keep their own job card while 12 per cent respondents reported that the job cards are kept with the PO and *Gram Panchayat*. The reporting from sample households clearly reveals existence of some irregularities and malpractice in issuance and entries in the job cards which are depicted in Table 2.13. This is a matter of serious concern in the study district.

Table 2.13: Qualitative Information Related Job Card

Perception on Job Card Issues	Description	Nos. of HHs (Figure in Parenthesis Represent Percentage)		
		Yes	No	Not sure
Job card issuance	Getting of Job card is simple and easy	14 (9.33)	102 (68)	34 (22.67)
	Paid any fees/charges etc., to get a job card	10 (6.67)	140 (93.33)	0(0)
Irregularity in the job card	No entries were made, even though the job card holder(s) had worked	16 (10.67)	122 (81.33)	12(8)
	Wrong entries or fake information entered in job card	16 (10.67)	122 (81.33)	12(8)
	Some entries had been over-written/manipulated	21 (14)	102 (68)	27(18)
Custodian of Job Card	With the card holders	132 (88)	NA	NA
	With *Gram Panchayat* officials	12 (8)	NA	NA
	Programme Officer	6(4)	NA	NA
	Elsewhere	0(0)	NA	NA
Knowledge about Job Card	Full knowledge	43 (28.67)	67 (44.67)	40 (26.67)

Source: Field Data

- *Application for Work Demanding:* Under MGNREGA, there is a provision to submit a written application for demanding employment to local authority stating time and duration of work. Local authority will issue a dated receipt for this written application. Employment will be given to applicants within 15 days of application, otherwise, daily unemployment allowance in cash has to be paid to concerned applicants.

The inquiry with beneficiary households reveals that in response to work application, 65.33 per cent households availed employment under MGNREGA. Out of total households which applied for works, 98 households get a dated receipt for the application whereas, 12 households were not given dated receipt. However, village level implementing authority failed to provide employment to 37 households within 15 days of application. Therefore, as per provision in the Act, unemployment allowance became due for payment to these 37 households. However, unemployment allowance due for payment was not paid so far to any one as depicted in Table 2.14. Therefore, the non-payment of unemployment allowance is a matter of great concern in the study district.

Table 2.14: Qualitative Information Related to Work Procedure of MGNREGA

Perception on Work Procedure	Description	Nos. of HHs (Figure in parenthesis represent Percentage)		
		Yes	No	Not sure
Work application	Employed by making application for work	98(65.33)	42(28)	10(6.67)
	Acquired dated receipt for the application	98(65.33)	12(8)	40(26.67)
	Employed within 15 days of application	78(58)	37(24.67)	35(23.33)
	Awarded unemployment allowance if not providing employment within 15 days	0(0)	37(24.67)	35(23.33)

Source: Field Data

- *Wage Payment Issues:* In respect of gender bias, 89.33 per cent participation households informed that no gender bias was seen in payment of wages for MGNREGA works. Only 4.67 per cent households reported that wage-rate is favouring men. Further, 70 per cent respondents reported their dissatisfaction about the existing wage rate under MGNREGA. Moreover, 83.33 per cent respondents commented on inequality between market wage rate and MGNREGA wage rate and 50.67 per cent respondents reported that there is no such mechanism to display wage rates at work site. The other issues relating to wage payment are depicted in the Table 2.15 which hints the existing practices of MGNREGA in the study district.

Table 2.15: Qualitative Information Related to Payment of Wages under MNREGA

Perception on Payment of Wages	Description	Nos. of HHs (Figure in parenthesis represent Percentage)		
		Yes	No	Not sure
Payment of Wages of MNREGA	Equal wage rates for men and women	134 (89.33)	7 (4.67)	9 (6)
	Satisfaction with Wage Rate	32(21.33)	105(70)	13(8.67)
	Wage Rate Equal to Market Rate	12(8)	125(83.33)	13(8.67)
	Displaying of Wage Rates Prominently	18(12)	76(50.67)	56(37.33)
	Compensation for Delayed Payment of Wages	143(95.33)	7(4.67)	0(0)
Period of wage payment	Paid within a fortnight	109(72.67)	41(27.33)	0(0)
	Paid within a month	36(24)	5(3.33)	0(0)
	Paid more than a month	5(3.33)	0(0)	0(0)
	Paid after one year	0(0)	0(0)	0(0)
Mode of wage payment	Payment at Bank/ PO account	132(88)	18(12)	0(0)
	Individual account	12(8)	6(4)	0(0)
	Joint account	6(4)	0(0)	0(0)
Complaints regarding wage payment	Delays in wage payments	102(68)	26(17.33)	22(14.67)
	Less wage than the minimum wage	11(7.33)	104(69.33)	35(23.33)
	Wage paid less than asked for sign/thumb impression	30(20)	98(65.33)	22(14.67)
	Faced problems in accessing post office/bank accounts	42(28)	88(58.67)	20(13.33)

Source: Primary Data.

- *Monitoring of MGNREGA Works:* To access the monitoring functioning of MGNREGA in the study district, 69.33 per cent households reported that either local or Block level authorities were found paying frequent flying visits at the worksites to monitor the execution of MGNREGA works (Table 2.16).

Except three household, no one lodge complaint relating to functioning of MGNREGA and supervisors at worksites. Though such practice shows satisfactory implementation and functioning of MGNREGA but still remains a question about the functioning. The discussion with villagers reveals that they had few complaints on functioning, wage measurement and wage payment of MGNREGA etc., but they lack courage and aptly remark that their complain will not entertain at all and present system could not be changed.

- *Usefulness of Works/Assets and Durability:* In respect of economic usefulness of the works executed under MGNREGA, 42.67 per cent beneficiary households believed that works were very useful to village community. However, at average 57.34 per cent considered it useful. This means that work plans and shelf of the projects prepared at village/block level reflect the needs and priority of the village community. Further, villagers expressed satisfaction for giving priority and inclusion of useful works under MGNREGA. Regarding the nature and durability of works, 25.33 per cent respondents çlaimed 'best and longer', 18 per cent respondents reported 'good', while 38 per cent reported 'average'. Only 18.67 per cent respondent reported the poor quality of the nature and durability of works undertaken under MGNREGA (Table 2.16).
- *MGNREGA Impact on Labour Migration:* One of the primary aims of MNREGA is to arrest out-migration of rural households in search of employment. With a view to know impact of MGNREGA on migration, related data were collected from the beneficiary households. The data reveals that after implementation of MGNREGA, out of 150 beneficiary households, 34 households (22.67%) reported the case of labour migration while 62 per cent reported 'no labour migration. This shows that after introduction of MGNREGA, migration continued because they felt limit of 100 days employment per household per year is quite inadequate for ensuring secured livelihood for the entire year. Further, 92 HHs (61.33%) reported that exactly 100 days of wage employment under MGNREGS is not at all provided. Moreover, 86 per cent reported that the present system of 100 days employment guarantee need to be increased and ensurement of guarantee needs to be in spirit (Table 2.16).

Table 2.16: Qualitative Information Related to Implementations Mechanism of MGNREGA

Perception on Implementation Mechanism	Description	Nos. of HHs (Figure in parenthesis Represent Percentage)		
		Yes	No	Not sure
Monitoring	Any authority to monitor the work	104(69.33)	11(7.33)	35(23.33)
	Any complaint lodged to the authorities	3(2)	147(98)	0(0)
	Any action taken against complain	0(0)	3(2)	0(0)
Economic usefulness of the works	Very useful projects	64(42.67)	74(49.33)	12 (8)
	Quite useful project	22(14.67)	32(21.33)	20(13.33)
	Not so useful to the villagers	10(6.67)	14(9.33)	8(5.33)
	Useless for the villagers	6(4)	0(0)	8(5.33)
Nature of assets and their durability	Good and longer	38(25.33)	NA	NA
	Not so good	27(18)	NA	NA
	Average	57(38)	NA	NA
	Poor	28(18.67)	NA	NA
How MNREGA has affected labour migration?	Family members migrated out for job after implementation of MGNREGA	34(22.67)	93(62)	23(15.33)
100 Days of Wage Employment	Exactly 100 Days of Wage Employment under MGNREGS is provided	21(14)	92(61.33)	38(25.33)
	100 Days of Wage Employment is sufficient	9(6)	129(86)	12(8)

Source: Field data

- *Awareness about MGNREGA:* Awareness on each and every aspects of MGNREGA among people is an important ingredient for success of MGNREGA. In surveyed villages, it was found that the people were aware about the implementation of MGNREGA programme but a large section of beneficiaries do not have full knowledge about the provisions of the Acts. However, probing of beneficiary households reveals that knowledge on various basic and rights based aspects such as:

right to unemployment allowance, wage calculation method, work application procedure, social-audit, wage-payment period, monitoring etc., was found limited, partly or negligible. Only 28.67 per cent households have full knowledge about the job cards, 32.67 per cent knew about application procedure for demanding work. Only 25.33 per cent beneficiary households had knowledge about right to minimum wages and level of minimum wages. As many as 84 per cent households were found unaware or unsure about their legal right to get unemployment allowance. Only 18.67 per cent households were aware about unemployment allowance but they were unaware about the rate of unemployment allowance. More than 51.33 per cent households were found unaware about provision of minimum facilities at worksite, mandatory availability of muster rolls at the worksite and permissible works under MGNREGA. Many were unaware about social audit and their role (Table 2.17).

Conclusion

From the above analysis and also from the secondary research studies, it is concluded that the performance of MGNREGA in Assam is not at all satisfactory. The scheme could not ensure the 100 days job guarantee to the majority of the job card holders in comparison to other north eastern states of India. Even we observed that the scheme fails in respect of providing employment avenues to the unemployed in a large scale. In fact the tune and essence of the Act could not satisfactorily implement in the State of Assam. Though MGNREGA there are positive impact on employment pattern of women but in Assam their participation is also low. The poor implementation across the nation (such as: lack of child care facility, worksite facility and illegal presence of contractors) accrued the gender sensitiveness of this Act mainly in north-eastern state of India. Certain initiatives and changes should be taken to remove these barriers. MGNREGA has been playing a significant role in human development. This act is very effective in addressing the problem of poverty in India which is the main cause of vulnerability of life. By generating income it has been act as a helpline in accessing social services for MGNREGA workers.

Table 2.17: Qualitative Information Related to Awareness about MGNREGA

Awareness Levels of Beneficiaries	Description	No. of HHs (Figure in Parenthesis Represent Percentage)		
		Yes	No	Not sure
Awareness	Full knowledge about Job Card	43(28.67)	67(44.67)	40(26.67)
	Employment provided under MGNREGS is a time-bound	43(28.67)	67(44.67)	40(26.67)
	Familiar with unemployment	28(18.67)	87(58)	35(23.33)
	allowance Eligibility of a person for unemployment allowance	28(18.67)	87(58)	35(23.33)
	Aware of the rate of wages under MGNREGS	43(28.67)	67(44.67)	40(26.67)
	Aware about MGNREGA implementation	125(83.33)	0(0)	25(16.67)
	Right to apply for work and get employed within 15 days	68(45.33)	47(31.33)	35(23.33)
	Aware about application procedure	49(32.67)	66(44)	35(23.33)
	Right to minimum wages	38 (25.33)	77(51.33)	35(23.33)
	Aware about level of minimum wages	38 (25.33)	77 (51.33)	35 (23.33)
	Right to the unemployment allowance	28(18.67)	87(58)	35(23.33)
	Mandatory availability of muster rolls at the worksite	38(25.33)	77(51.33)	35(23.33)
	List of permissible works under the MGNREGA	38(25.33)	77(51.33)	35(23.33)
	Minimum worksite facilities (drinking water, first aid,)	38(25.33)	77(51.33)	35(23.33)
	Social audit	38(25.33)	77(51.33)	35(23.33)

Source: Field Data.

But the poor implementation across the nation and in Assam in particular (such as: demand side deficiencies, delay and violations preparatory steps violation of democracy and transparency in planning, failure to ensure registration and issue job cards, violation of norms for work, non-payment of minimum wages and unemployment allowances, delayed payments, lack of worksite facility and illegal presence of contractors etc.,) accrued the right-based approach of this act. Certain initiatives and changes should be taken to check the loopholes of the Act. For this purpose Government, civil society, local communities, *Panchayati Raj* Institutions etc., should take proper initiatives in its planning and implementation. The valuable gains should not be derailed for poor implementation.

Recommendations

The MGNREGA is a new life line of the rural people who earn their livelihood as wage earners. It also gears up the social relationship among the rural people which is a pre requisite condition to build a strong society or a nation. It also reduces the gender difference for some works which are in practice in rural areas. Some suggestions are incorporated here on the basis of survey of literature.

(a) All the programmes under MGNREGA must be well planned well ahead of time with a definite time frame for completion.

(b) State MGNRGEA has much more to do to strengthen the *Panchayati Raj* System, curtailment of direct intervention of other departments or agencies associated with it, would be a welcome step in this regard.

(c) Present target of 100 days employment per house hold should be ensuring strictly.

(d) Wage rate should have parity with outside rate and ongoing price hike which would reduce the migration of labour from village to nearby township or city.

(e) More transparency is needed about the sanctioned work and financial involvement therein.

(f) Auditing may be done through an extra government agency in addition to *Gram Panchayat* to check mishandling of fund.

(g) *Panchayat* should be empowered financially and job responsibility should be distributed to all the elected members.

(h) Any kind of political intervention should be stopped.

(i) Strengthening active citizenship is a must.

(j) Build large scale citizen's awareness campaigns for generating demand side of MGNREGA.

(k) Improve institutional capacities of Gram *Panchayat*.

(l) Financial Inclusion – Banks and Insurance network must be extended.

(m) People's participation through *Gram Sabhas* needs to be ensured.

(n) Social Audits for transparency and accountability is a must.

(o) Access to Information at every stage of implementation is quite necessary.

(p) IT platform for placing all information in public domain.

(q) Innovative use of ICT for development of financial products needs to be implemented.

(r) An effective grievance redressal mechanism needs to be evolved.

(s) Partnerships with Academia, Media, Legal Fraternity, Financial Institutions is quite necessary.

NOTES

1. North East Social Trust Report (2013). Report of MGNREGA in Assam. Retrieved from http://www.nestinfo.org.
2. Ministry of Home Affairs (2011). Programmes undertaken in North Eastern Region by the Ministry of Information and Broadcasting, Government of India, Newsletter, Vol. XIII, No. 8.
3. MGNREGA MIS Report (2012). Available at http://nrega.nic.in/netnrega/MISreport3.aspx?fin_year
4. Ministry of Rural Development (2013). MGNREGA Sameeksha: An Anthology of Research Studies on MGNREGA, Chapter 1.
5. CRISIL Research Insight (2012). MGNREGA report, August. Retrieved from http://crisil.com/pdf/economy/research-insight_ rural-consumption_ Aug12.pdf
6. Ministry of Rural Development (2012). MGNREGA Sameeksha, Chapter 5.
7. Ministry of Rural Development (2012). MGNREGA Sameeksha, Chapter 5.
8. North East Social Trust Report (2013). MGNREGA report. Retrieved from http://www.nestinfo.org.
9. Ministry of Rural Development (2013). Union Ministry for Rural Development Report to the people on MGNREGA. Retrieved from http://nrega.nic.in/netnrega/WriteReaddata/circulars/Report_to_ the_people_ English2013.pdf.
10. CAG Report (2007). Performance Audit of Implementation of National Rural Employment Guarantee Act, 2005, Draft Report, New Delhi: Comptroller and Auditor General.
11. National Rural Employment Guarantee Act (2005). Operational Guideline 2008, loc. cit., p. 61.
12. National Rural Employment Guarantee Act (2005). Schedule-1, Paras-6 to 8.

REFERENCES

1. Adhikari, Anindita and Kartika Bhatia (2010). NREGA Wage Payments: Can We Bank on the Banks? *Economic and Political Weekly*, 5(1), 30-37.
2. Akthar, S.M., Jawed and Abdul, Azeez N.P. (2012). Rural Employment Guarantee Programme and Migration, *Kurukshetra*, February, 60(4), 11-15.
3. Ambasta, Pramathesh, Vijay Shankar, P.V. and Shah, Mihir (2008). Two years of NREGA: The Road ahead, *Economic and Political Weekly*, 43(8), 41-50.
4. Bardhan, Kalpana (2011). Rural Employment, Wages and Labour Markets in India: A Survey of Research - III, *Economic and Political Weekly*, 12(28), 1101-1118.
5. Bhatia, Bela and Dreze, Jean (2006). Employment Guarantee in Jharkhand: Ground Realities, *Economic and Political Weekly,* July 22, XLI (29), 3200-3202.
6. Bhowmik, Indraneel (2013). MGNREGS in Tripura: A Study on Efficiency and Equity, V.V. Giri National Labour Institute, NLI Research Studies Series. No 102/2013. Retrieved from http://www.vvgnli.org/sites/default/files/publication_files/MGNREGS%20in%20Tripura.pdf.
7. Bordoloi, Jotin (2011). Impact of NREGA on Wage Rates, Food Security and Rural Urban Migration - A Study in Assam, Study No. 138 Agro-Economic Research Centre for North East India, Assam: Assam Agricultural University.
8. Borgohain, Rupa Barman (2005). Guaranteeing Employment: A Bold Vision. The Assam Tribune. March 13. Retrieved from http://www.assamtribune. com.
9. CAG Report (2007). Performance Audit of Implementation of National Rural Employment Guarantee Act, 2005, Draft Report, New Delhi: Comptroller and Auditor General.
10. Chakraborty, P. (2007). Implementation of the National Rural Employment Guarantee Act in India: Spatial Dimensions and Fiscal Implications. *Working Paper No. 505,* Annandale-on-Hudson, NY: The Levy Economics Institute.
11. Chandrasekhar C.P. and Ghosh, J. (2005). Social Inclusion in the NREGS, Business Line (India), January 27.
12. Chhabra, S., Raina, R.L., and Sharma, G.L. (2009). *A Report on Management of National Rural Employment Guarantee Scheme: Issues and Challenges*. Delhi: Lal Bahadur Shastri Institute of Management.
13. Chowdhury, Subhanil (2012). Employment in India: What Does the Latest Data Show, *Economic and Political Weekly*, December 31, XLVI (53), 26-32.
14. CRISIL Research Insight (2012). MGNREGA report, August. Retrieved from http://crisil.com/pdf/economy/research-insight_rural-consumption_Aug12.pdf
15. Das, Basanti (2007). Governmental Programmes for Rural Development, New Delhi: Discovery Publishing House Pvt. Ltd.

16. Das, Dinesh (2012). Examining India's Mahatma Gandhi National Rural Employment Guarantee Act: Its Impact and Women's Participation, *International Journal of Research in Management*, November, 6(2), 209-218.
17. Dreze, J. and Khera, R. (2009). The Battle for Employment Guarantee. *Frontline*, 26(1), 4-26. [Online]. Available: http://info.worldbank.org/etools/docs/library/245844/Public%20workdThe%20battle%20for%20employment%20guarantee.pdf [04/06, 2011].
18. Dreze, J., Khera, Reethika and Sidharth (2007). NREGA in Orissa: Ten loopholes and the silver lining; Interim survey report (mimio), *Survey conducted by G.B Pant Science Institute.*
19. Dreze, Jean (2008). Employment Guarantee Act: Promise and Demise. In Berma, Sawalia Bihari; Upadhya, Yogesh and Sant Gyaneshwar Pd. Singh (Ed.), Rural Employment. New Delhi: Sarup and Sons.
20. Gaiha, R., V.S. Kulkarni, M.K. Pandey and K.S. Imai (2009). National Rural Employment Guarantee Scheme, Poverty and Prices in Rural India, *ASARC Working Paper no*. 2009/03, ASARC.
21. Gopal, K.S. (2009). NREGA Social Audit: Myths and Reality, *Economic and Political Weekly*, January, 44(3), 70-75.
22. Goswami, H.K. (2008). NGRGA: A Powerful Weapon, The Assam Tribune, April 18. Retrieved from http://www.assamtribune.com.
23. Goswami, H.K. (2009). NGRGA Implementation in Andhra Pradesh. The Assam Tribune, October 15. Retrie ed from http://www.assamtribune.com.
24. Haberfeld, Y., Menaria, R.K., Sahoo, B.B. and Vyas R.N. (2011). Seasonal Migration of Rural Labour in India, *Population Research and Policy Review*, 18(5), 473-489.
25. Harrison, Fidel Ezeala (2011). Analysis of Wage Formation Processes in Rural Agriculture, *The Journal of Developing Areas*, 38(1), 79-92.
26. Hazarika, P.G (2009). Promoting Women Empowerment and Gender Equality through the Right to Decent Work: Implementation of National Rural Employment Guarantee Programme (NREGP) in Assam State (India) - A Case Study, International Institute of Social Studies. The Hague, Netherlands. Retrieved from http://knowledge.nrega.net/1100/2/FINAL_RP_Pranati.pdf.
27. Hirway, I. and Saluja, M.R. (2009). Engendering Public Works Programme by Addressing Unpaid Work of Women in Developing Countries Case Study in India, New Delhi: National Workshop on NREGA and Women's Empowerment.
28. Indira Hirway, and Neha Shah (2011). Labour and Employment under Globalisation: The Case of Gujarat, *Economic and Political Weekly*, May 28, XLVI (22), 57-65.
29. Jacob, Arun and Varghese, Richard (2006). NREGA implementation - I: Reasonable Beginning in Palakkad, Kerala, *Economic and Political Weekly*, December 02, XLI (48), 4943-4945.

30. Jandu, B. (2009). NREGA in India. Retrieved from http://www.righttofood india.org/Data/nrega-a-people's-act-a%20revolutionary-step.pdf
31. Jeyaranjan, J. (2011). Women and Pro-Poor Policies in Rural Tamil Nadu: An Examination of Practices and Responses, *Economic and Political Weekly*, October 22, XLVI (43), 64-74.
32. Jha, R., Gaiha, R., and Shankar, S. (2008). Reviewing the National Rural Employment Guarantee Programme, *Economic and Political Weekly*, 43(10), 44-48.
33. Jha, R., Gaiha, R., and Shankar, S. (2009). National Rural Employment Guarantee Programme in Andhra Pradesh and Rajasthan: Some Recent Evidence, *Contemporary South Asia,* 18 (2), 205-213.
34. Jha, Raghbendra and Raghav Gaiha (2012). REGS: Interpreting the Official Statistics, *Economic and Political Weekly*, XLVII (40), 18-22.
35. Jha, Raghbendra, Gaiha, Raghav and Shankar, Shylashri (2009). Capture of Anti-poverty Programmes: An Analysis of the National Rural Employment Guarantee Programme in India, *Journal of Asian Economics*, Elsevier, 20(4), 456-464.
36. Kar, Spandita (2013). Empowerment of Women through MGNREGS: Issues and Challenges, *Odisha Review*, February – March, 76-80.
37. Khandelwal, Varun and Chawla, Kanika (2006). NREGA and Rural India, eCatalyst, Feb, Vol. 7. Retrieved from http://www.ccsindia.org/ccsindia/ec7/ec7_varun.htm
38. Khera, R. and Nayak, N. (2009). Woman Workers and Perceptions of the NREGA, *Economic and Political Weekly*, 44, 49-57.
39. Khera, Reetika (2008). Empowerment Guarantee Act, *Economic and Political Weekly*, August 30 – September 05, XLII (35), 8-10.
40. Khera, Reetika and Karuna, Muthiah (2010). Slow but Steady Success, The Hindu, April 25.
41. Khera, Reetika and Nayak, Nandini (2009). Women Workers and Perceptions of Rural Employment Guarantee Act, *Economic and Political Weekly*, 64(43), 49-57.
42. Krishnamurthy, J. (2006). Employment Guarantee and Crisis Response, *Economic and Political Weekly*, March 04, XLI (9), 789-790.
43. Kumar, P. (2011). Impact of NREGA on Wage Rate, Food Security and Rural-Urban Migration in Karnataka. Project Completion Seminar. Delhi: Institute for Social and Economic Change.
44. Louis, Prakash (2006). NREGA Implementation II - Birth Pangs in Bihar, *Economic and Political Weekly*, December 02, XLI (48), 4943-4946.
45. Mahapatra, Jugal K (2008). Rural Employment Guarantee. In Berma, Sawalia Bihari; Upadhya, Yogesh and Sant Gyaneshwar Pd. Singh (Ed.), *Rural Employment,* New Delhi: Sarup and Sons.

46. Mehrotra, Santosh (2008). NREG Two Years On: Where do we go from here? *Economic and Political Weekly*, August 2-8, XLIII (31), 27-35.

47. Ministry of Rural Development (2013). Union Ministry for Rural Development Report to the people on MGNREGA. Retrieved from http://nrega.nic.in/netnrega/WriteReaddata/circulars/Report_to_the_people_English2013.pdf.

48. NCAER-PIF (2009). Evaluating Performance of National Rural Employment Guarantee Act, Project Report. Retrieved from http://www.ncaer.org/downloads/Reports.

49. North East Social Trust Report (2013). MGNREGA report. Retrieved from http://www.nestinfo.org.

50. North East Social Trust Report (2013). Report of MGNREGA in Assam. Retrieved from http://www.nestinfo.org.

51. Panda, B. and Umdor, S. (2011). Appraisal and Impact Assessment of MGNREGA in Assam, Shillong: North - Eastern Hill University.

52. Panda, B., Dutta, A. K. and Prusty, S. (2009). Appraisal of NREGA in the States of Meghalaya and Sikkim, Indian Institute of Management, Shillong. Retrieved from http://www.nrega.net/pin/.../NREGA-IIMShillong-Final%20Report.pdf

53. Patel, Amrit (2006). Role of PRIs in Implementing Rural Employment Guarantee Scheme, *Kurukshetra*, August, 54 (10), 24-25.

54. Patra, Sudhakar and Dhal, P.C. (2009). Rural Development and National Rural Employment Act. In Dash, Gyanindra and Sahoo, Rajan Kumar (Ed.), *Rural Employment and Economic Development*, New Delhi: Regal Publications.

55. Puja Dutta, Rinku Murgai, Martin Ravallion, Dominique van de Walle (2012). Does India's Employment Guarantee Scheme Guarantee Employment? *Economic and Political Weekly*, April 21, XLVIL(16), 55-64.

56. Puri, Manuhar (2008). The NREGA: Rural People to Grow with the Nation. In Berma, Sawalia Bihari; Upadhya, Yogesh and Sant Gyaneshwar Pd. Singh (Ed.), *Rural Employment*, New Delhi: Sarup and Sons.

57. Rai, Parsuram (2010). Dalits of Bundelkhand Living with Hunger and Dying of NREGA Mafia, Centre for Environment and Food Security.

58. Raja, A. (2007). Ensuring the Right to Work for Women: A Review of NREGA from the Gender Perspective. In: *Gender and Governance: Reviewing the Women's Agenda in the National Common Minimum Programme*. Delhi: Wada Na Todo Abhiyan.

59. Raju, V.T. (2011). The Impact of New Farm Technology on Human Labour Employment, *Indian Journal of Industrial Relations*, 11(4), 439-510.

60. Ramesh, G. and Kumar, T.K. (2009). Facet of Rural Women Empowerment: A Study in Karimnagar District in Andhra Pradesh, *Kurukshetra*, 58, 29-30.

61. Ravindranath, N.H., and Tiwari, R. *et al.* (2009), *Environmental Services and Vulnerability Reduction through NREGA; Findings of the Rapid Assessment in Chitradurga District of Karnataka.* Bangalore: Centre for Sustainable Technologies, Indian Institute of Science.
62. Saha Roy, Chhanda (2013). Right Based Approach in Accessing Social Sector Services - A Case Study of MGNREGA, *Global Research Methodology Journal*, Feb-Mar-Apr, II, 8. Retrieved from http://www.grmgrlaranya.com/Journals/8th%20issue/7.pdf, accessed 1 February 2013.
63. Sankaran, Kamala (2011). NREGA Wages: Ensuring decent work, *Economic and Political Weekly*, 66 (7), 23-25.
64. Sankaran, Kamala (2011). NREGA Wages: Ensuring Decent Work, *Economic and Political Weekly*, February 12, XLVI (7), 34-39.
65. Scandizzo, P., Gaiha, R. and Imai, K. (2009). Option Values, Switches and Wages: An Analysis of the Employment Guarantee Scheme in India, *Review of Development Economics,* 13 (248-263).
66. Shah, Deepak (2012). Implementation of NREGA in Maharashtra: Experiences, Challenges and Ways Forward, Munich Personal RePEc Archive MPRA, Paper No. 39270. Retrieved from http://mpra.ub.uni-muenchen.de/39270
67. Shah, Mihir (2007). Employment Guarantee, Civil Society and Indian Democracy, *Economic and Political Weekly*, 42(45 and 46), 43-51.
68. Shamsi, A. Nayyer (2007). National Rural Guarantee Act, *Competition Refresher*, November, XXV (11), 36-39.
69. Shrinivasan, Rukmini (2012). NREGA's Non-existent Impact on Migrant Labourers. The Times of India, June 28. Retrieved from http://timesofindia.indiatimes.com.
70. Siddhartha and Vanaik, Anish (2008). CAG Report on NREGA: Fact and Fiction, *Economic and Political Weekly*, June 21-27, XLIII (25), 39-45.
71. Singh, J.N. and Mishra, Anurag (2006). Backward Linkages of Rural Employment Guarantee Scheme", Kurukshetra, August, 54(10), 30-35.
72. Singh, Puran (2008). National Rural Employment Guarantee Scheme – A Task Ahead. In Berma, Sawalia Bihari; Upadhya, Yogesh and Sant Gyaneshwar Pd. Singh (Ed.), *Rural Employment*, New Delhi: Sarup and Sons.
73. Singh, S. (2009). NREGS: Issues of Governance and Transparency. Report prepared for Commonwealth University London. Jaipur: Institute of Development Studies.
74. Thomas, E.C. (2008). Job Guarantee for Rural Poor. In Berma, Sawalia Bihari; Upadhya, Yogesh and Sant Gyaneshwar Pd. Singh (Ed.), *Rural Employment*, New Delhi: Sarup and Sons.
75. Tiwari, Rakesh, Somashekhar, H.I., Ramakrishna, V.R., Murthy, Indu K., Mohan Kumar, M. S., Mohan Kumar, B.K., Parate, Harshad, Verma, Murari, Malaviya, Sumedha, Rao, Ananya S., Sengupta, Asmita, Kattumuri,

Ruth and Ravindranath, N.H. (2011). MGNREGA for Environmental Service Enhancement and Vulnerability Reduction: Rapid Appraisal in Chitradurga District, Karnatka, *Economic and Political Weekly*, 66 (20), 39-47.

76. Trivedi, B.R. and Aswal, B.S. (2011). Encyclopedia of NREGA and Panchayati Raj, New Delhi: Cyber Tech Publications.
77. Vanaik, Anish and Siddhartha (2008). Bank Payments: End of Corruption in NREGA? *Economic and Political Weekly,* April 26, XLIII (17), 33-39.
78. Vijayakumar, B. and Thomas, S. N. (2008). Governance, Institutions and National Rural Employment Guarantee Scheme, International Conference on *NREGS in India: Impacts and Implementation Experiences*, New Delhi, September 16-17.
79. Zorlu, Aslan and Hartog, Joop (2003). The Effect of Immigration on Wages in three European Countries, *Journal of Population Economics*, 18(1), 113-151.

Pages: 57-66

Rural Economy: ***Changing Landscape***

Edited by: **Dr. Kartick Das**

ISBN: 978-93-5056-838-5

Edition: **2017**

Published by: **Discovery Publishing House Pvt. Ltd., New Delhi (India)**

3 Microfinance and Rural Development
Potentialities of Panchayati Raj Institutions

— **Kartick Das**

For a country such as: India, with 850 million people living on less than $2 (Rs. 97) a day, it is relevant to talk about creating avenues for those who struggle for the basics. Foreseeing the need for structural change, Muhammad Yunus of Bangladesh popularised the concept of Microfinance, and the world today beholds a Grameen Bank serving over 7.34 million people with a recovery rate of 98.35 per cent.[1] Microfinance refers to the provision of financial services to low-income clients, including consumers and the self-employed. More broadly, it refers to a movement that envisions a world in which as many poor and near-poor households as possible have permanent access to an appropriate range of high quality financial services, including not just credit - it includes other financial services as:

- Savings.
- Insurance.
- Fund transfer.
- Remittances.
- Risk mitigation products.
- Financial counseling.
- Lifecycle planning products.

Democracy and development occupied top priority in the agenda of state and societies in the past Second World War period. The denial of substantive democracy and development accounts for the growth of various social and economic conflicts and ailments in India. The author is of the view that democratic decentralisation of power is essential for ensuring development in the country. But regrettably it is noticed that by the late 1960s the benefits of rapid growth did not reach the rural poor and the gap between the rich and the poor became wider and wider. So the idea of people's participation in the process of development gained momentum and development became broad - band. So far as the rural development our country is concerned, the Panchayati Raj Institutions (PRIs) accordingly to the author if economically empowered can extend micro credit to the rural poor and encourage them to undertake various economic activities resulting in to a spectacular change in the standard of their living. In this context the author refers to Sri Aurobindo and Mahatma Gandhi who were staunch advocates of Panchayati Raj. In the backdrop of post-independence India's rural development experience up to early 1980s the major thrust of which were 'development from above' the 73rd and 74th Constitution Amendment Acts, 1993, have for the first time brought about a change in it by giving priority to the people's participatory role in the process of rural development *i.e.*, 'development from within'. Though these Amendment Acts have vested the PRIs with substantive administrative and judicial powers (Article – 243 and 11th Schedule) but did not provided effective financial power which could have been used in rural development. The author opines that the PRIs if financially empowered could have been a successful agency for extending micro credit to the poor in the villages. The potentialities of the PRIs in bringing about rural development through the management of micro credit extension have remained so far unexplored.

Objective

The major objectives of the proposed study:

1. To examine the frequent shift in thrust and approach of rural development and public policy in the post-independence India.
2. To explore the potentialities of the PRIs (the third tier of democratic governance after the constitutionalisation of the PRIs by the 73rd and 74th Constitution Amendment Acts, 1993) to became an effective micro finance institution at the door steps of the rural poor.

3. To highlight the role of people's participatory approach in all development initiatives leading to the empowerment of the rural masses.
4. To suggest measures as to how the PRIs can become a successful nodal agency of rural development.

Methodology

The paper is based exploration and descriptive analysis and the observations are made therein depending upon the author's personal experience gathered through interaction with the villages and their elected representatives to the village panchayati named the Pub-Lumding Gaon Panchayat, Lumding, Nagaon, Assam.

Changing Role of Panchayati Raj Institutions

Rural development in the context of India is essentially an attempt in improving the living condition of the rural poor. The growth maximisation was the centre of development policies of the Third World Countries in the 1950s and early 1960s and the bureaucracy was viewed as the instrument of development. But by the late 1960s it was noticed that the benefits of rapid growth did not ultimately reached the poor and the gap between the rich and the poor were widened due to the impact of so-called rapid growth. These developments have brought about a shift in the concept and strategy of rural development, slogans like: 'growth with social justice' or 'redistribution with growth' etc., became very popular and the idea of people's participation in the process of development also gained momentum. This shift of emphasis has made development broad-based.

Sri Aurobindo said "(In India) one should begin with the old panchayat system in the villages and the work up to the top. The panchayat system and guilds are more representative and they have a living contact with people; they are the part of the people's ideas."[2] But it was Gandhiji who moved for the first time in the 20th century India, the idea of reviving the Panchayati Raj Institutions (PRIs). These bodies would have democratic bases of their own vested with adequate powers so that the villagers could have a real sense of swaraj and ensure rural development. This move of Gandhiji resulted in the introduction of Article 40 in the Constitution of India which states that "the state shall take steps to organize village panchayats and endow them with such powers and authority as may be necessary to enable them to function as units of self-government". This article formed a part of the Directive Principles of State Policy under the Constitution. However, the new government immediately enacted no legislation to implement the Article 40.

The post-independence India embarked on rural development through the Community Development (CD) and National Extension Services (NES) Programme in 1950s. The programme was a multi-purpose open-ended programme. It failed to achieve its development objectives. Moreover, this programme was officially sponsored programme imposed from the top and were not designed to evoke people's initiative. The Balavanta Rai Mehta Committee recommended the introduction of three-tier elective panchayat for ensuring peoples participation giving scope for structural variation at the provincial level. But the PRIS did not strike grassroots. The lack of political and partisan interest coupled with bureaucratic neglect crippled the PRIs. Moreover, adequate funds and functions were not given to them. After this the Ashoka Mehta Committee was appointed in 1977 for suggesting ways and means of reviving the PRIs.

During 1970s the development thrust shifted to the target group like: small and marginal farmers and development bodies as exemplified by the creation of the Small Farmers Development Agency, The Marginal Farmers and Agricultural Development Agency were created. Moreover, area-specific special developmental programmes like: The Command Area Programme, The Drought Prone Area Programme were launched to end regional imbalances. As a result of the implementation of the above programmes the role of bureaucracy also regained momentum once again because the funds were transferred directly to the bureaucratic agencies by passing the PRIs. In this way the beneficiaries became the recipients rather than active participants in the process of rural development. This approach *i.e.,* 'Rural Development from the above' continued in subsequent Five-year Plan documents; only the emphasis went on getting shifted. The Sixth Five-year Plan has for the first time introduced the Integrated Rural Development Programme (IRDP) which seeks to provide the poor families with income-generating assets. The District Rural Development Agency (DRDA), a new body for channel zing the central funds was created, which also by passed the PRIs and sponsored the bureaucratization of the rural development process in

India. The National Rural Employment Programme (NREP), the Rural Landless Employment Guarantee Programme (RLEGP). The Jawahar Razgar Yojana (JRY), The National Rural Employment Guarantee Act (NREGA), The Swarnajayanti Gramin Sawrojgar Yojana (SGSY) etc., launched during the subsequent Five-year Plan period the major thrust of which were income-generation to eradicate rural poverty.

The concept of people's self-participatory approach in the institutions for rural development *i.e.,* the PRIs began to attract serious attention of policy-makers since the mid-1980s. In the wake of the enactment of the 73rd and 74th Constitutional system, now, the PRIs have attained a statutory status being vested with the substantial administrative and adjudicating power (Article 243) The PRIs are considered 'Third Tier' of the Government in our federal structure of polity in all purposes specially in matters of administration of justice protection of rights of the people, public welfare and rural development. It is a matter of concern, even after the constitutionalisation of the PRIs the bureaucracy continues to play a big role in Members of Parliament (MPs) Area Development Scheme after the passing of the above Constitution Amendment Acts such funds are also utilized through the District Collectors/Deputy Commissioners. The DRDA is still headed by the District Collector in most of the provinces except a few like: West Bengal and Karnataka.

Surprisingly, even after the constitutionalisation of the PRIs (73rd and 74th Constitution Amendment Acts, 1993) the PRIs do not have any effective power in the direct management of micro credit which is considered to be a crucial instrument of income generation, poverty alleviation, and above all provision of economic empowerment to the rural poor. The Part-IX (The Panchayats) and Part-IXA (The Municipalities) of the Constitution which contains Article 243 bears the clauses from 243A to 243Z, interestingly, do not empower the PRIs to become an agency of micro credit/finance for rural development. Furthermore, the 11th Schedule (Article 243G) of the Constitution which deals with the detailed list of powers and functions of the PRIs also do not confer any power upon the PRIs to become a crucial agency/institution of micro credit/finance for rural development. Although there is ample scope under the existing system for the PRIs to play a more effective role in extending micro credit for rural development that the government, non-government commercial and other credit extending agencies, yet the potentialities of the PRIs so far remained unexplored.

The PRIs can become a feasible alterative to the existing government and non-government Micro Finance Institution (MFIs). The flow of capital of the PRIs may be maximized if the existing system of fragmentation and sharing of centrally sponsored rural development fund is discontinued and in its place major share of it may be directly injected to the PRIs. Fragmentation of funds among different government and non-government Agencies/Institutions is a major deterrent in the way of poverty alleviation, empowerment of the rural poor, and is responsible for piece-meal or scattered approach to rural development. If the policy of direct injection of funds to the PRIs is implemented whole heartedly the shortage of capital of the PRIs may be minimized and they will get larger scope of empowering the rural poor and could ensure overall rural development. In this connection the NGOs, educational Institutions and expert agencies may be engaged as consultants in the matters of capacity building exercise and training of the Self-help Groups and officials of the PRIs.

The PRIs particularly the Gaon Sabha can play the role of an institution for single-window clearing system and can simplify the existing complex norms of sanctioning and disbursement of loans to the rural poor and Self-Help Groups (SHGs). The excess of conditionality as insisted by the Banks and other MFIs in times of sanctioning the loans blockades the entrepreneur ventures of the rural poor/SHGs and thereby impede the empowerment of the rural masses and overall rural development. The Gaon Sabha also can adopt area-specific simplified norms particularly in tribal villages where the people practice their traditional customary rules and regulations. Moreover, the Gaon Sabha can effectively monitor and supervise the progress of the projects and can provide necessary help to the SHGs to overcome any difficulty in the post-sanction period of the project. The Gaon Sabha can easily provide the required pre-sanction and post-sanction viability/feasibility reopen on the projects as it is well-versed with the capacity, skill, and behavioural pattern of all the village flock. The Gaon Sabha also can act as a collective guarantor of the rural poor and SHGs and can easily recover the outstanding loan amount in case of default as the beneficiaries easily cannot escapc from the locality and the fear of loosing the future dose of loans to there. In this way the Gaon Sabha can minimise the problem of bad debts as frequently encountered by the MGIs.

Measures

The following measures may be suggested to make the PRIs an effective MFI for rural development.

- The PRIs should be empowered through legislation to become an agency/institution to provide micro credit. The scheme may be named as the Panchayati Raj Microfinance Scheme.
- The Gaon Sabha may be empowered to act as the pioneering organ of PRIs in the matter of pre-sanctioning and post-sanctioning of loans to the rural poor and SHGs. (The service of the Gaon Sabha may be engaged in selecting the proposed beneficiaries, preparing the beneficiary list, examining the viability of the project/activity/scheme, deciding the loan amount, making the repayment schedule, supervision and monitoring of the project, timely recovery of the advance and getting all these matters approved in the Gaon Sabha meeting).
- The seed capital to start the Panchayati Raj Microfinance Scheme shall provided by the Finance Commission to be constituted as per the provisions of Article 243-I.
- To eradicate the maladies of fragmentation of centrally sponsored funds the Planning Commission must directly allocate the funds directly to the PRIs.
- The PRIs should identify all the skilled personhoods engaged in various activities available in the village area and organize them into SHGs or Societies and register them accordingly to get economic benefit.
- The PRIs should provide equal opportunity to the women and backward classes in all developmental schemes.
- The Gaon Sabha should ensure the contribution and participation of people in all developmental activities.
- The PRIs should constitute a Village Panning Body or Committee from among the villagers in the Gaon Sabha meeting to plan for the economic development of the village.
- The accounts of the Panchayati Raj Microfinance Scheme may be kept open to the Gaon Sabha and may be available for public audit.

- The PRIs should endeavour to make the office of the Panchayat and information centre and an agency for co-ordination with the government and non-government institution.
- The government should adopt a policy to open branches of different government departments like: Revenue, Soil Testing, Soil Conservation, P.H.E., Medical Centre, Veterinary Centre, Seed Farm, Sericulture and Horticulture Centre, Sericulture Centre, Bank Branch etc., in the village so that the villagers may get the necessary help in the door steps of the village.

It can be said that in the aftermath of the 73rd and 74th Constitution Amendment Acts the development of PRIs, for people's self-participatory institution for rural development is constitutional requirement. They should be given utmost priority by both the public policy-makers and planners as well. But our experience shows that these institutions did not grow evenly in all parts of the country due either to the existence of traditional local factor or structural inadequacies in the Acts concerned. Now the time has come to give up the concept of 'development from above' and accelerate the 'development from within' or 'initiative from bases up to top' by which the PRIs may move towards self-reliant small republics in Indian federal polity. To quote Gandhiji "The village republic will be managed by a Panchayat which will be a living potential force and entity. Panchayats will be united in a free and voluntary association by even widening circle of a village republic. It will not be an apex sustained by the bottom but an oceanic circle whose centre will be the individual, always ready to perish for the circle of villages and so on, sharing the majesty of the oceanic circle which they are parts."[3]

Concluding Remarks

Microfinance is not yet at the centre stage of the Indian financial sector. The knowledge, capital and technology to address these challenges however now exist in India, although they are not yet fully aligned. With a more enabling environment and surge in economic growth, the next few years promise to be exciting for the delivery of financial services to poor people in India. Microfinance will continue to develop into an important delivery mechanism to reach out to the poor and achieving financial inclusion and empowerment of women. Its role in enhancing human capital is considerable. The objective of the microfinance initiatives must be to evolve the bankable clients to creditworthy clients, thus making concerns about poverty irrelevant. To conclude, people should be empowered in all respects to become self-reliant, they should not be treated as humble recipients but active participants in all developmental initiatives. The beneficiaries are no more patients but they are active agents of rural development. In this connection the late Prime Minister Rajib Gandhi once said, "We trust the people, we have faith in the people. It is the people who must determine their own destinies and the destiny of the Nation. To the people and India, let us ensure maximum democracy and maximum devolution. Let the people be empowered."[4]

NOTES

1. Interview of Muhammad Yunus, Published in Yojana, January 2008, pp. 7-9.
2. See Booklet (2002). Rajib Gandhi Chair for Panchayati Raj Studies, Department of Political Science and Development Administration Gandhigram Rural Institute, Gandhigram, Tamil Nadu, p. 2.
3. Ibid., p. 2.
4. Ibid., p.1.

REFERENCES

1. Government of India Publication Division, Civil Line, Delhi - 110054: The Constitution of India (as on 1st June, 1996).
2. Kohli Atul (ed.): The Success of India's Democracy: Cambridge University Press, Foundation Books Pvt. Ltd., 4764/2A, 23 Ansari Road, New Delhi, 110002, 2004.
3. Chattterjee Partha (ed.): State and Politics in India: Oxford University Press, YMCA Library Building, New Delhi - 110001, 2008.
4. Chatterjee Partha: The Partha Chatterjee Omnibus: Oxford University Press, YMCA Library Building, New Delhi - 110001, 2008.
5. Rao V.V. and Niru Hazarika: A Century of Government and Politics in North East India: Vol. I (Assam) (1874-1980): S. Chand and Co. Ltd., New Delhi - 110055, 1991.
6. Ahuja Ram: Society in India: Rowat Publiations, Jaipur - 302004, 2003.
7. Ahuja Ram: Social Problems in India: Rowat Publication, Jaipur - 302004, 2002.
8. Mahashwari, S.R.: Local Government of India, L.N. Agarwal Educational Publishers, Agra - 3, 2000.
9. Bhattacharyya Mohit: Public Administration: The World Press Pvt. Ltd., Calcutta, 1987.

10. Basu, D.D.: Introduction to Constitution of India: Wadhawa and Co, Law Publishers, New Delhi, 2003.
11. Rajib Gandhi Chair for Panchayati Raj Studies: Department of Political Science and Development Administration Gandhigram Rural Institute – Deemed University. Gandhigram - 624302, Tamil Nadu.
12. Good Governance at the Grassroots: Department of Political Science and Development, Gandhigram Rural Institute – Deemed University, Gandhigram - 624302, Tamil Nadu.
13. The Role of Women Members in the Decision-Making Process of the Local Self-Governing Institutions of Assam: A Case Study of Pub-Lumding Gaon Panchayat – Micro Research Project Conducted by the Department of Political Science, Lumding College, Lumding, Assam, 2004.
14. Prime Minister's Speech on 'Ditiya Seuj Biplober Dishot' (Towards the Second Green Revolution) at the National Krishi Vigyan Kendra Sanmilon, 27-28, October, 2005. New Delhi: DAVP Ministry of Information and Broadcasting, Government of India, New Delhi, February, 2006.
15. Prime Minister's speech on 'Nirman' EK Unnato Bhavishat at the Hindustan Times Leadership Summit, 15th November, 2005, Delhi: DAVP Ministry of Information and Broadcasting, Government of India. New Delhi, February, 2006.
16. N.E. News letter: Vol. 8 No. 3 – March, 2006: N.E. Division Ministry of Home Affairs, North Block, New Delhi, 11001.
17. PRIs and Development of Assam: Dr. U.N. Bora: The Assam Tribune, Monday, January 6, 2003: The Tribune Press, Gauhati.

Pages: 67-87

Rural Economy: *Changing Landscape*
Edited by: **Dr. Kartick Das**
ISBN: 978-93-5056-838-5
Edition: **2017**
Published by: **Discovery Publishing House Pvt. Ltd., New Delhi (India)**

Potential of MGNREGA in Empowering Rural Women
A Case Study in Nagaon District in Assam

— **Sanjay Kanti Das**

INTRODUCTION

Generally a person is said to be empowered if s/he acquires command and control over resources, access to education, healthcare that enhances their capability, knowledge, skill, productivity and thereby improve their social status, self-confidence and participation in various decision-making and political processes. In other words, empowerment is the ability of an individual to gain control socially, politically, economically, and psychologically through *(a)* access to information, knowledge, and skills *(a)* decision-making; and *(c)* individual self-efficacy, community participation, and perceived control (Zimmerman and Rappaport, 1988).

Empowerment is a multi-dimensional process, which should enable people to realise their full identity and power in all spheres of life (Surekharao and Rajamanamma, 1999). It consists of greater access to knowledge and resources, greater autonomy in decision-making to enable them to have greater ability to plan their lives, or to have greater control over the circumstances that influence their lives (Indiresan, 1999). Empowerment is the feeling that activates the psychological energy to accomplish one's goals. Generally, true process of development is expected to generate the forces that lead to empowerment of various sections of population in a country and to raise their status especially of women. Looking at the above mentioned definitions of empowerment, it is imperative to analyse how participation of people in MGNREGA leads to their empowerment among the women flock.

Asymmetry in gender relations at household and society levels in social, economic and political spheres in rural India has been a critical issue for all development professionals. It has become a critical barrier in achieving the avowed goal of economic growth with social justice. The declining sex ratio is an indication of the gender disparities in our societies. In other words, a high sex ratio is construed as a favourable sign of a progressive society and one expects that men and women enjoy equal status in all domains of development (Dheeraja *et al.* 2010). The prevalence of these desirable conditions including participation of women in decision-making holds great promise of empowerment of women. Different socio-economic and political instruments interventions have been launched during the last six decades to bring harmony in the gender relations, of course varying degrees of success. The Mahatma Gandhi National Rural Employment Guarantee Act (MGNREGA) is one such intervention in the labour market with built in gender bias in favour of women, as an affirmative action for bringing about a semblance of equality. The participation of women in the aforesaid programme in India is shown in the below Fig. 4.1.

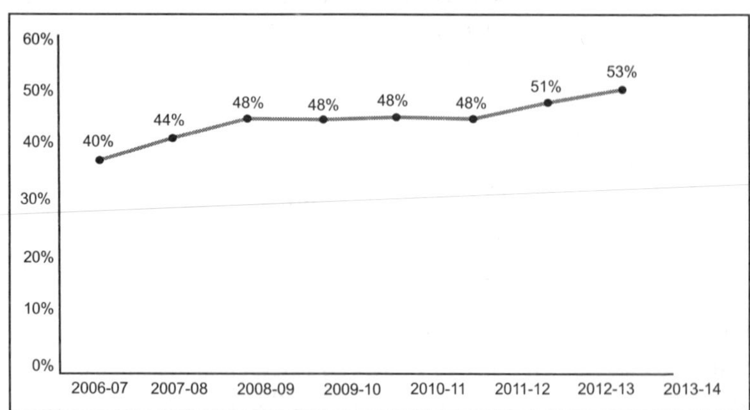

Fig. 4.1: **Women Participation in MGNREGA**

Source: MGNREGA official website

An important objective of MGNREGA has been to encourage women's effective participation, both as workers and as administrators. For instance, according to MGNREGA guidelines, at least one-third of the beneficiaries shall be women who have registered and requested for work under the programme. Further, since employment is provided within 5 km., radius of the village, it has the potential to bolster women's participation. The 68th round of NSSO data[1] shows that between 2004-05 and 2011-12, there has been a negative trend in women's labour force participation rate in rural India. Rural female participation fell from nearly 25 per cent in 2004-05 to 21 per cent in 2009-10 and then even lower to around 17 per cent in 2011-12. However, a study by Mehtabul (2012) using nationally representative National Sample Surveys (NSS) data found that MGNREGA has helped to mitigate the situation. The study exploited the phase-wise expansion of the MGNREGA and found that the decline in labour force participation in MGNREGA districts has been lower than the decline observed in non-MGNREGA districts. This effect is found to be more pronounced in the case of female labour participation. Significantly, female share of works under MGNREGA is greater than their share of work in the casual wage labour market across all states (Dutta, Murgai, Ravallion and Dominique, 2011; Shivakumar and Mallikarjun, 2015). Women are participating in the scheme much more actively than they participated in other forms of recorded work (Ghosh, 2009; Dheeraja and Rao, 2010).

MGNREGA's own official data shows that women's participation in MGNREGA has been on the rise. At the national level, it increased from 40 per cent in 2006-07 to 53 per cent in 2013-14. However, there are wide variations across states and across districts within a state. While the statute mandates that at least one-third of the beneficiaries shall be women, the actual proportion varies, ranging from 22 per cent in Uttar Pradesh to 93 per cent in Kerala in 2013-14. The southern states like: Kerala, Tamil Nadu and Andhra Pradesh show a higher rate of participation (Dutta, Murgai, Ravallion and Dominique, 2011). Among the northern and some eastern states, however, the pattern has been low, with Rajasthan and Himachal Pradesh being the exceptions. The interstate variations in women participation can be attributed to a host of factors ranging from socio-cultural norms around female participation in labour force, mobility and intra household allocation of roles and responsibilities, opportunity costs in terms of wage differentials between private sector and MGNREGA, efficiency of implementing institutions at the State and local government levels and influence of Self-Help Groups and NGOs

(MGNREGA Sameeksha [2]; Dheeraja and Rao, 2010; Sorsa, 2015). For instance, in the case of Kerala, where MGNREGA has turned out to be an almost 'ladies only' affair, the fact that Kudambashree (a State government initiative for poverty eradication through networking of women's groups) has been placed in charge of its implementation has also made a striking difference to the level of women's participation. This convergence has played its part in evolving the economic identity of the rural woman - as skilled labourer and farmer cultivator. It has also created a development interface for women to negotiate with local governments and power structures, giving new meaning to participatory governance. In Rajasthan, active youth groups and other social movements have been deeply involved and encouraged women participation in the programme. As a result, general levels of awareness are much higher than they would have been if advocacy had been left exclusively to the district administration (Dutta, Murgai, Ravallion and Dominique, 2011). Under MGNREGA, the clause of equal pay for men and women has also been adhered to and has resulted in shaping out a better socio-economic scenario for rural women of India. The NSSO 66th round data brings out the clear gender wage gap in unskilled wages. This difference was much larger in other public works; 98.3 per day for men and 86.1 per day for women. Such gender wage gaps are high across the country and among the highest in Kerala and Tamil Nadu. The NSSO data shows that MGNREGA has reduced the traditional wage discrimination in public works. Women therefore, have looked upon MGNREGA, where minimum wages are to be paid, as a viable alternative. This may explain to an assured extent, the higher women participation in states where the initial condition in unskilled agriculture work is more imbalanced between men and women. An interesting example is that of Kerala which has the highest gender wage gap in agricultural labour and also the highest participation rate in MGNREGA[3].

Improved access to economic resources and paid work has had a positive impact on the socio-economic status of women. Studies (Ghosh, 2009) indicate that women exercise independence in collection and spending of MGNREGA wages, indicating greater decision-making power within the households. Women have also reported better access to credit and financial institutions. The mandatory transfer of wage payment through bank accounts has ensured a greater financial inclusion of women. Despite these improvements, certain factors such as: non-availability of work-site facilities like: creches, long work hours, gender relations, implementation challenges continue to occlude women's full participation. Functional and safe mobile creche services, flexibility in terms of women's working hours and provision for gender-specific life cycle needs are likely to provide women with more time and opportunity to participate actively in MGNREGA. This would be an important step in narrowing down the prevalent gender gap in rural India.

Participation as a Process of Empowerment

In the process of rural development the term participation and empowerment are considered to be positively correlated. The entire community development programmes implemented so far aim at empowering the communities and improving the quality of their lives. But, at the same time it has also been realised that it is impossible to achieve this goal without active participation and involvement of the community in the projects meant for them. Friedman (1992) emphasised on people's active participation in their development projects that would contribute to their level of empowerment. The study also stated that the local government has an important role in this regard to promote better living conditions for the whole community with active participation and possible initiatives of the community.

Community developments concern the creation of improved social and economic conditions through voluntary cooperation and self-help efforts of the communities and participation is a vital component of the self-help process and community development (Javan, 1998). In other words, people must be involved in those decisions that affect their lives, thus gain in confidence, self-esteem, knowledge, and develop new skills Bharthamma (2005). Nikkah and Redzaar (2009) also stress that empowerment for the poor can be achieved only when they have active participation in the process of development. According to Ahmed et al (2011) in Bangladesh with participation of women in micro credit programme have gained much empowerment in terms of self confidence and decision-making capacity.

MGNREAGA Implementation in India

MGNREGA has been one of the issues for discussion among the social scientist since its implementation. Various studies were made in different period of time, touching the various aspects of MGNREGA. Recent study by Manoj (2011) has looked into the problems and prospects of MGNREGA in India and has suggested a number of remedial strategies to tide over the problem. Another very recent study by Manoj (2012) has looked into the utmost significance of ICT based tools for effective implementation of MGNREGA, including prevention of the possible misuse of the funds under the scheme using the potential of ICT advances. Prasad (2012) highlighted the different objectives and features of MGNREGA and also revealed the performance and funding pattern of MGNREGA. According to his study MGNREGA is playing vital role for providing employment especially during off agricultural season. Borah and Bordoloi (2014) conducted their study on impact of MGNREGA on women empowerment in Sonitpur district of Assam and concluded that the performance of MGNREGA is not fully satisfactory. The scheme could not ensure the 100 days job guarantee to the majority of job card holders in the studied district. Kumar (2014) attempted to explain the importance of social audit in developmental schemes like MGNREGA in Haryana. They observed that most of the gram panchayat has conducted social audit twice in a year. Sharma (2014) explained the reasons for migration in urban and rural area and how MGNREGA can be an effective tool for reducing such migration. Hazarika (2014) examined the impact of MGNREGA on income and migration of people of Lakhimpur District, Assam and observed that scheme has a positive impact on eradicating poverty by increasing income of people and decreasing the rural migration.

The implementation of MGNREGA has got tremendous potential to bring about far reaching improvements in the socio-economic life of the rural poor. The implementation of MGNREGA could be observed to be a boon to unemployed rural women in India, as it can enhance the socio-economic and political empowerment of rural women. It may be noted that in spite of the fact that Assam has got one of the best profiles of socio-economic and educational achievements in the whole of India, the state is having a very high unemployment rate. This is turn enhances the prospects of MGNREGA in Assam, particularly with respect to rural women. However, though there is high development potential, MGNREA implementation in Assam has been facing a number of problems and challenges. In the above context, this paper looks into the efficacy in empowering rural women, along with its major problems and prospects; by making an empirical study at Nagaon district of Assam.

Table 4.1: Performance of MGNREGA in Assam and Nagaon District of Assam

	Assam				Nagaon			
Total No. of Districts	27							
Total No. of Blocks	238	18						
Total No. of GPs	2,640	235						
Total No. of Job Cards [In Lakhs]	43.62	2.62						
Person days Generated so far [In Lakhs]	FY 2015-16	FY 2014-15	FY 2013-14	FY 2012-13	FY 2015-16	FY 2014-15	FY 2013-14	FY 2012-13
FY 2015-16 Women Person days out of Total (%)	144.66 30.55	210.89 28.13	298.47 24.75	314.04 26.01	25.06 20.55	39.46 18.82	41.53 16.25	31.01 15.39

Source: MGNREGA Public Data Portal[4]

Women through MGNREGA

As a rural wage employment programme, MGNREGA recognised the relevance of incorporating gender equity and empowerment in its design. Various provisions under the Act and its Guidelines, aim to ensure that women have equitable and easy access to work, decent working conditions, equal payment of wages and representation on decision-making bodies. The NREGA with its guarantee of 100 days of unskilled work for every household has been envisaged as gender sensitive scheme'. The main way in which a scheme for social protection can to be made gender sensitive is to suggest that a certain percentage of beneficiaries must be women, which have been provided for in the Act: 'While providing employment, priority shall be given to women in such a way that at least one-third of the beneficiaries shall be women who have registered

Table 4.2: Parameters of MGNREGA in Assam and Nagaon District of Assam

	District Name	Total Job Cards Issued	Total Households Demanded Work	Total Persons Demanded Work	Total Households Worked	Total Persons Worked	Total Person Days Worked	Total Person days Worked by Women	Total Households Reached 100 day Limit
2012-13	NAGAON	2,16,445	95,521	1,01,545	95,234	1,01,135	31,01,237	4,77,297	3,456
	ASSAM	40,10,637	12,47,461	14,87,274	12,34,828	14,72,543	3,14,03,828	81,69,143	9807
2013-14	NAGAON	2,29,812	1,16,434	1,26,336	1,11,835	1,20,898	41,52,560	6,74,888	4,315
	ASSAM	41,15,872	13,21,079	16,01,573	12,61,778	15,25,443	10,02,346	73,87,470	15,505
2014-15	NAGAON	2,45,922	1,29,305	1,44,276	1,18,964	1,31,707	39,46,418	7,42,850	3,204
	ASSAM	42,21,515	10,83,473	13,87,741	9,66,980	12,24,039	2,10,88,655	59,33,280	10,449
2015-16	NAGAON	2,50,858	1,03,866	1,16,209	91,482	1,01,889	25,29,685	5,15,129	1,339
	ASSAM	42,56,925	8,89,703	11,72,275	7,22,323	9,41,012	1,46,57,326	44,19,357	4,099

Source: MGNREGA Public Data Portal[5]

and requested for work under the scheme (National Rural Employment Guarantee Act: 2005; Schedule II, Section 6: 19). The Act also provides for some explicit entitlements for women to facilitate their full participation. These include:

- *Equal wages for men and women*: Equal wages shall be paid to both men and women workers and the provisions of Equal Remuneration Act, 1976 shall be complied with.
- *Participation in management and monitoring of the programme*: As per the guidelines, a local Vigilance and Monitoring Committee is to be appointed with members from the immediate locality or village where the work is undertaken, to monitor the progress and ensure the quality of work. The gram sabha/panchayat will elect the members of the committee and ensure that SCs/STs and women are represented on it.
- *Participation in social audit*: The guidelines mention about social audit forum, convened by the 'gram sabha/panchayat' every six months as part of the continuous auditing process. There is stress on the quorum of these meetings maintaining female participants alongside those from other disadvantageous groups. The timing of the forum must be such that it is convenient for people to attend - that it is convenient for Rural Employment Guarantee Scheme workers, women and marginalised communities (Narayanan, 2008).
- *Providing support for child care, and convenience to households*: The guidelines mention that the need for a creche at the worksite, and for the works to be convenient for families. If some applicants have to be directed to report for work beyond 5 kms., of their residence, women (especially single women) and older persons should be given preference to work nearer to their residence. Also, if several members of a household who share the same job card are employed simultaneously under the scheme, they should be allowed to work on the same work site.
- *Ensuring that single woman is eligible*: By recognizing a single person as a 'household', the Act makes it possible for widows and other single woman to access work.

MGNREGA plays a significant role to meet the practical as well as strategic needs of women's participation. It has become a beacon of light in the empowerment of the rural women and contributed substantially for the increased living and economic conditions by creating equal wages to male and female workers. The role of MGNREGA on women's participation can be examined through the following parameters (Kar, 2013):

(i) *Income-consumption effects*: By income-consumption effects we mean an increase in income of women workers and as a result, their ability to choose their consumption baskets. MGNREGA empowers women by giving them a scope of independent earning and spend some amount for their own needs.

(ii) *Intra-household effects:* Women play a major role in raising the economic resources for their family but their contribution remains uncounted because of they perform a significant amount of unpaid work. In rural areas, the dominance of males in intra-household decisions has been seen. MGNREGA has significant impact in converting some unpaid work into paid work and widen the scope of decision making role of women in household matters.

(iii) *Community-level effects:* Women's participation at the local and district level of governance process is low in spite of 73rd Amendments of the Constitution. But women participation has increased after the implementation of MGNREGA in many areas. A large number of women workers attended the Gram panchayat meeting held in connection with MGNREGA. Community level empowerment of women is one of the great achievements of this Act.

Issues Related to Women Participation in MGNREGS

MGNREGS act stipulates that wages will be equal for men and women. It is also committed to ensuring that at least 33 per cent of the workers shall be women. By generating employment for women at fair wages in the village, MGNREGA can play a substantial role in economically empowering women and laying the basis for greater independence and self-esteem. However MGNREGA also suffers from some serious limitations:

(i) *Non-availability of child care facilities*: One of the major shortcomings of the Act is non-availability of proper crèche facilities at the work site even though the Act includes this provision. Different studies show that women remained worried

about their children while they are working at MGNREGA worksite even some women do not accept the job facilities of MGNREGA because of non-availability of proper child care facilities.

(ii) *Low level of awareness:* In Assam women participation is low because of low level of awareness about the process and entitlements of the programme. Many of the male folks have withdrawn from agricultural activities and joined works in MGNREGA. This vacated space in agriculture has been occupied by the womenfolk and this scene is in study areas.

(iii) *Nature of work:* Most of the studies reveal that nature of work is also not helpful for women workers. In most of the projects selected being related to rural connectivity and renovation of local water bodies involving earth work requiring application of physical force, male workers were preferred to women workers (Hazarika, 2009).

(iv) *Poor worksite facilities:* MGNREGA funds have been allocated for the provision of safe drinking water, resting place and first aid. But most of the studies reported that except drinking water facility all other facilities are generally absent.

(v) *Delay in payments:* Delay in payments is also responsible for poor participation of women particularly in case of single women if they are the main earners in the family. Because the Banks are far from the village, it becomes difficult for the women to open Bank Account and draw cash which discourage women participation.

Objectives of the Study

- To make a critical analysis of the potential of MGNREGA in bringing about socio-economic and political empowerment of rural women, including the problems faced by them, based on a field study at Nagaon district in Assam.
- To offer meaningful suggestions for more effective implementation of MGNREA based on the findings of the field study.

Methodology of the Study

The study is both descriptive and analytical. It is descriptive to the extent that it seeks to narrate the salient features including major issues and challenges in the implementation of MGNREGA with special reference to Assam. The study is analytical too as it makes a critical analysis of the potential of MGNREGA in bringing about socio-economic and political empowerment of rural women including analysis of the major problems faced by them. The data used are both secondary and primary. Secondary data are collected from authentic sources like: Government publications such as: Economic Review, Economic Survey, NSSO estimates etc. Primary data are collected using a carefully designed, pre-tested Questionnaire from the 200 women workers understudy who is chosen at random from workers engaged in MGNREGA. Popular tools of statistical analysis are used to analyse and interpret the data collected as above.

Profile of Rural Women Workers Under NREGS

As already noted there are 200 rural women workers in the sample selected for the study, cutting across different religions and castes. A brief discussion on the socio-economic and demographic profile of these women workers in the sample is given below.

Table 4.3: Age Profile of the Sample of Women Workers (MGNREGS)

Particulars	Profile of the Rural Women Workers			
	Below 35	35 to 50	Above 50	Total
No. of workers in each group	76	90	34	200
Percentage Share	38	45	17	100

Source: Field Survey

It is noted that 38 per cent of the workers are below 35 years, 45 per cent within 35-50 years and the rest 17 per cent above 50 years. Thus, middle-aged (35-50 years) people account for relatively larger share in the sample workers under study as it is as high as 45 per cent (Table 4.3).

Table 4.4: Religious Composition of the Workers

Hindu	52%
Muslim	47%
Christian	1%

Source: Field Survey

From Table 4.4 it is noted that majority of the workers are from the Hindu religion and they account for 52 per cent of the total. Second are the Muslim women workers who account 47 per cent of the workers.

Women Empowerment Potential of MGNREGA

For assessing the women empowerment potential of MGNREGA by means of a field study, the following factors from the three important aspects women empowerment like economic empowerment, political empowerment and social empowerment have been considered: *(i)* Better Financial planning and discipline, *(ii)* Freedom to spend and save the earnings, *(iii)* Freedom from money lenders and bankers, *(iv)* Deciding on purchase of household goods, *(v)* Freedom to decide on children's education, *(vi)* Raising voice against injustice, *(vii)* Expressing opinion in meetings/discussions, *(viii)* Election campaigning/contesting in elections, *(ix)* Public speaking ability. Suitable weights are attached to the responses of the respondents under study *viz*; Weight 2 for 'Yes', Weight 1 for 'To Some Extent', and Weight 0 for 'No' (Table 4.5). Now, the factors leading to women empowerment can be categorized based on their empowerment potential into three major group *viz*; High Empowerment, Moderate Empowerment and Low Empowerment as shown below:

- Average Score below 0.67 – Low Empowerment.
- Average Score between 0.67 to 1.33 – Moderate Empowerment.
- Average Score above 1.33 – High Empowerment.

From Table 4.5, it is observed that MGNREGA has got an appreciably high level of potential for women empowerment. This is evidences from the high overall (total) score of 1.34 considering all the nine factors together. Besides, it is noted that the economic empowerment potential is the highest as evidenced by the very high scores of the first three individual factors and also a very high average score of 1.70 for the three factors taken together. In respect of social empowerment too, the overall potential for empowerment is high at the level of 1.37; and among the three individual factors in this group the factor 'Deciding on purchase of household goods' has got a very high (eventually the highest among all the nine factors under study) score of 1.86, followed by another factor 'Freedom to decide on Children's education' with a very high score of 1.63 while the third factor 'Raising voice against injustice' has got a rather poor score of 0.63. In respect of political empowerment, the average score for the three factors put together (0.95) as well as the individual scores for the three different factors are quite moderate. In short, it may be pointed out that MGNREGA implementation has given rise to very high level of

Table 4.5: Potential of MGNREGA for Women Empowerment

Empowerment Constructs	Factors related to Socio-Economic and Political Empowerment of Women	Level of Empowerment			Total Score (weighted score of 810 Employee Seach)	Weighted Average Score
		Yes (Weight 2)	To Some Extent (Weight 1)	No (Weight 0)		
Economic Empowerment	Better Financial planning and discipline	163	32	5	358	1.79
	Freedom to spend and save the earnings	153	40	7	346	1.73
	Freedom from money lenders and bankers	123	67	10	313	1.57
	Total	1017	1.70			
Social Empowerment	Deciding on purchase of household goods	174	23	3	371	1.86
	Freedom to decide on children's education	134	58	8	326	1.63
	Raising voice against injustice	45	25	120	125	0.63
	Total	822	1.37			
Political Empowerment	Expressing opinion in meetings/discussions	97	33	70	227	1.14
	Election campaigning/ contesting in elections	44	77	79	165	0.83
	Public speaking ability	47	83	70	177	0.89
	Total		569	0.95		
	Total				2408	1.34

Source: Field Survey.

economic empowerment, high level of social empowerment and quite moderate level of political empowerment of rural women.

The summary position of the relative empowerment scope of the nine factors under study is shown in Table 4.6. Accordingly, it is noted that MGNREGA has got high potential for empowering rural women in 5 vital aspects (factors) while it has got moderate potential for empowerment of rural women in respect of 3 other factors, and its potential is quite low in respect of one factor.

Table 4.6: Categorization of Factors based on their Potential for Women Empowerment

High Potential	Moderate Potential	Low Potential
1. Better Financial planning and discipline,	1. Expressing opinion in meetings/discussions,	1. Raising voice against injustice
2. Freedom to spend and save the earnings,	2. Election campaigning/ contesting in elections,	
3. Freedom from money lenders and bankers,	3. Public speaking ability	
4. Deciding on purchase of household goods,		
5. Freedom to decide on children's education		

Source: Field Survey.

Further Discussion on Women Empowerment Potential of MGNREGA

Economic Empowerment of Women due to MGNREGS is reviewed from angles like: Employment Opportunity, Women as Wage Earner, Wage Parity, Control rights of Women in Earning from MGNREGA, Financial Inclusion, and Bargaining Power:

- *Employment opportunity*: MGNREGA contains provisions which cater to the laudable objective of socio-economic empowerment of women with respect to wages and work opportunity. So far as women participation in MGNREGA in Assam is concerned, the women participation rate in Assam is 26.01 per cent in 2012-13 over 30.5 per cent in 2015-16. The separate accounts of women have also been open in the State. In district Nagaon the women participation rate is 15.39 per cent in 2012-13 which rose to 20.55 per cent in 2015-16. The participation rate of women is currently in increasing trend in the district but it is low owing to delayed wage payment. Still one fact is clear that some improvement has started owing to improvement in wage payment system and using time and motion study to determine the quantum of work per day.

- *Women as wage earner*: The MGNREGS has helped in the women becoming wage earner. The wages earned contribute to the family income, which is used for clothing, nutrition and health care of the members. The MGNREGS employment of women has helped them to play a parity role in decision-making.
- *Wage parity*: There is no gender discrimination with regard to minimum wage rate prevalent under MGNREGA in the state of Assam and they are being paid equal wages for equal work. Keeping in view the anatomical features of rural folks of Assam, productivity norms have been rationalized with relation to nature of soil, depth of digging, etc., for which clear norms exist in the State.
- *Control rights of women in earning from MGNREGS*: The women workers are becoming economically empowered due to MGNREGS. They get the wages through the system of bank account payments or through post office, which gives them the control right on their earning. Women now earn equally so they have also started taking interest as to how their earning is to be utilised.
- *Financial Inclusion*: 'No fill bank account' was opened for the payment of MGNREGS wages. This Increased transparency in payments and also encouraged the habit of thrift and savings. This has had the greatest impact on women workers for whom financial independence was a dream. The indebt analysis based on secondary data shows that 100 per cent of workers had bank accounts from among the registered workers and about 100 per cent of wage payment is through accounts (Bank/Post Office).
- *Bargaining power*: The bargaining power of women workers have improved due to MGNREGS projects. The average wage rate in the agriculture sector also went up toward minimum wages. Previously, women worked were poorly paid. Now with MGNREGS, the general wages for women has increased in all types of work. The total household income has also increased as now women are able to work in MGNREGS Scheme during lean agricultural season and undertake agriculture activity during agricultural period.

Social empowerment of women cannot be quantitatively measured but the impact of it can be qualitatively felt. The important qualitative changes are in the form of changed attitude to work, social acceptability, happiness and contentment. Social empowerment of women due to MGNREGS is reviewed from angles like: Social interaction, Women participation in social audit, Participation in decision making, Dignity of labour, and Impact on education and health sectors:

- *Social interaction*: MGNREGS has brought social interaction between different social groups and have also brought interaction between men and women. They now work shoulder to shoulder to earn their dignified living. The social dogmas which restricted the genders to work together have gone out. The caste divide has also ended, which is a great advantage of MGNREGS.
- *Women participation in social audit*: Women participation in social audit is being encouraged by the government but it has not gained much ground. Formation of social audit team is lacking and so is the women participation in social audit.
- *Participation in decision-taking*: The women workers are being encouraged to participation in decision-taking. The formation of Self-Help Groups and Participation of women at the Panchayat level as elected members has given them strength to highlight the issues which are prime for social well-being.
- *Dignity of labour*: Through implementation of the scheme in the right earnest, the status of the workers improved and dignity of labour was ensured. For the first time the worker could demand work and get his dues in a time bound and transparent manner. This has transformed the relationship between the work provider and the worker from that of a master servant relationship to one of an employer and an employee. Ensuring dignity of labour has probably been one of the most important outcomes of MGNREGS.
- *Impact on education and health sectors*: It is a well known fact that increasing incomes of the poor lead to better retention rates in schools and a greater chance of continued education for children. The observation in Nagaon districts of Assam has shown a positive impact on education. The data from the field shows that there has been a substantial reduction in dropout rates in primary schools in

the district. The MGNREGS has ensured employment to the poor in rural India. The MGNREGS was implemented to give livelihood to the poor families. The survey reveals that in some schemes the enrolment of the women is higher.

Confidence and self-esteem of the women: The 'Woman' earns the wages for 100 days in a dignified manner without being harassed by contractors etc. There is a definite rise in the confidence and self-esteem of the women. They are vocal and also conscious of their rights. (Job cards, wage rate, days of work etc.) This has brought out the quality of "Leadership amongst the women especially those from the backward sectors. The MGNREGS generate employment identified sectors. The main indented schemes are related to land works, forestry programmes, fisheries, agriculture, floriculture, horticulture, irrigation etc., when a woman is employed in these schemes she gains knowledge, about the various things and soon exercises her opinion in decision taking regarding choice of plans.

Concluding Remarks and Suggestions

In view of the foregoing, it may be opined that Kerala has got excellent potential to become a role model for the entire nation for systematic and corruption-free implementation of MGNREGA. The strong presence of the poverty alleviation programme of the State Government *viz*; 'Kudumbashree' has made the position of MGNREGA implementation in this state unique; ensuring high level of effectiveness and transparency unlike in most other states in India. The field study has shown that there is quite high level of potential for MGNREGA for socio-economic empowerment of women, and reasonable (moderate) level of political empowerment too. The experience so far being satisfactory, the Kerala's model of MGNREGA implantation could replicated in other states. The Act appears to be quite meaningful and powerful for rural development in general and women empowerment in particular for the entire nation. The problem lies not in the Act per se, but in its defective implementation and lack of proper monitoring; as is evident from the bad experiences and unhealthy practices. Involvement of the middlemen, political and bureaucratic exploitation, misuse of funds, muster roll manipulation, lack of transparency etc., need to be strictly controlled. The prospects of the MGNREGA for rural development and women empowerment are quite bright provided it is properly executed. Though the vital causes of suffering shown above are before our eyes these can be reduced easily if the schemes and its execution are reviewed frequently and in such cases if lapses are seen they should be immediately rectified. Regarding this, the followings suggestions are given:

- The employees related with the schemes should be devoted, dutiful and they must have positive vision of their own.
- State MGNRGEA has much more to do to strengthen the Panchayati Raj System, curtailment of direct intervention of other departments or agencies associated with it, would be a welcome step in this regard.
- The circle administration should be brought down to village level or lower level so that all the development programmes under MGNREGA can reach the villages situated at a distance from Development Block.
- Auditing may be done through an extra government agency in addition to Gram Panchayat to check mishandling of fund.
- Panchayat should be empowered financially and job responsibility should be distributed to all the elected members.

NOTES

1. Retrieved from http://www.academia.edu/4828689/Employment_Trends_in_India_An_Overview_of_NSSOs_68th_Round
2. Retrieved from http://nrega.nic.in/netnrega/writereaddata/circulars/mgnrega_sameeksha.pdf
3. Success stories – MGNREGA. Retrieved from http://nrega.nic.in/netnrega/writereaddata/circulars/convergence_mgnrega_story_jan_2014_eng.pdf.
4. Retrieved from [http://mnregaweb4.nic.in/netnrega/dynamic2/dynamicreport_new4.aspx]
5. Retrieved from [http://mnregaweb4.nic.in/netnrega/dynamic2/dynamicreport_new4.aspx]

REFERENCES

1. Ahmed, F., Siwar, C. and Idris, A.H (2011). Woman Empowerment through Participation in Micro credit Programme: A Case Study, *American Journal of Applied Science,* 8(9), 878-883.
2. Bharathamma (2005). Empowerment of Rural Women through Income Generating Activities in Gadag district on Northern Karnataka, Thesis submitted to the University of Agricultural Science, Dharwad.

3. Borah, K. and Bordoloi, R. (2014). MGNREGA and its Impact on Daily Waged Women Workers: A Case Study of Sonitpur District of Assam, *IOSR Journal of Economics and Finance*, 4 (4), 40-44.
4. Dheeraja, C., Siva Ram, P. and Rao, H. (2010). Changing Gender Relations: A Study of MGNREGS across Different States, Hyderabad: National Institute of Rural Development (NIRD).
5. Dutta, Murgai, Ravallion and Dominiquc (2011). Does India's Employment Guarantee Scheme Guarantee Employment.
6. Friedman (1992). *Empowerment: the Politics of Alternative Development*, Blackwell Publisher Ltd., Oxford, U.K.
7. Ghosh, J. (2009). Equity and Inclusion through Public Expenditure: The Potential of the NREGS, New Delhi: Paper for International Conference on NREGA, 21-22 January 2009.
8. Hazarika, P.G. (2009). Promoting Women Empowerment and Gender Equality through the Right to Decent Work: Implementation of National Rural Employment Guarantee Programme (NREGP) in Assam State (India): A Case Study.
9. Idiresan, J. (1999). Empowering Women Challenge to Educational Institutions, Paper Presented in *National Conference on Empowerment of Women for National Development*, Dhole, 15-19.
10. Javan, J. (1998). Empowerment for Community Development: A Multivariate Framework for Assessing Empowerment at the Community Level, Department of Psychology, North Carolina State University.
11. Kar, Spandita (2013). Empowerment of Women Through MGNREGS: Issues and Challenges, Odisha Review, February – March, 76-80.
12. Kumar, V. (2014). Social Audit in MGNREGA: A Case Study of three Districts of Haryana, *Shiv Shakti International Journal in Multidisciplinary and Academic Research*, 3 (3), 177-181.
13. Manoj P.K. (2011). MGNREGA Implementation in India: Problems, Prospects and Remedial Strategies with Special Reference to Kerala, In P Arunachalam (Ed.), Mahatma Gandhi National Rural Employment Guarantee Programme and Poverty in India, New Delhi: Serials Publications.
14. Manoj P.K. (2012). Information and Communication Technology (ICT) for Effective Implementation of MGNREGA in India: An Analysis, In P Arunachalam (Ed.) (145-150), Digital Economy of India – Security and Privacy, New Delhi: Serials Publications.
15. Mehtabul Azam (2012). The Impact of Indian Job Guarantee Scheme on Labor Market Outcomes: Evidence from a Natural Experiment, World Bank, IZA DP No. 6548 (May). Retrieved from http://ftp.iza.org/dp6548.pdf
16. Narayanan, S. (2008). Employment Guarantee, Women's Work and Childcare. *Economic and Political Weekly*, March 1, 10-13.

17. Nikkhah, H.A. and Redzuan, M. (2009). Participation as a Medium of Empowerment in Community Development, *European Journal of Social Science*, 11(1), 170-177.
18. Prasad, K.V.S. (2012). Performance of Mahatama Gandhi National Rural Employment Gurantee Act (MGNREGA): An Overview, International *Journal of Management and Business Studies*, 2 (4), 99-103.
19. S. Hazarika (2014). MGNREGA and its Impact on Migration in Lakhimpur district of Assam, *Vision NE*, 1 (2), 116-126.
20. Sharma, A. (2014). MGNREGA - An Alternative to Migration, *Kurukshetra*, 62 (11), 26-28.
21. Shivakumar S. Sangan and Mallikarjun J. Akki (2015). Mahatma Gandhi National Rural Employment Guarantee Scheme and Women: An Overview, Review of Research, 4(5), 1-12. Retrieved from www.ror.isrj.org
22. Sorsa, Piritta (2015). Raising the Economic Participation of Women in India: A New Growth Engine? OECD Economics Department Working Papers. Retrieved from http://www.oecd-ilibrary.org/economics/raising-the-economic-participation-of-women-in-india_5js6g5kvpd6j-en?crawler=true.
23. Sudarshan (2009). India's National Rural Employment Guarantee Act Women's Participation and Impacts in Himachal Pradesh, Kerala and Rajasthan.
24. Surekharoa, K. and Rajanananna, J. (1999). Empowerment of Rural Women through DWCRA Programme, Paper Presented in *National Conference on Empowerment of Women for National Development*, Dhole, 101-107.
25. Zimmerman, M. and J. Rappaport (1988). Citizan Participation, Perceived Control and Psychological Empowerment, *Amercian Journal of Community Phsychology*, 16(5), 725-750.

Pages: 88-103

Rural Economy: *Changing Landscape*
Edited by: **Dr. Kartick Das**
ISBN: 978-93-5056-838-5
***Edition:* 2017**
***Published by:* Discovery Publishing House Pvt. Ltd., New Delhi (India)**

MGNREGA in West Bengal
An Employment Security of Rural Informal Labourers

— **Rathindra Nath Pramanik**

INTRODUCTION

According to the National Commission of Enterprise in the Unorganized Sector (NCEUS), 'the informal sector consists of all unincorporated private enterprises owned by individuals or households engaged in the sale and production of goods and services operated on a proprietary or partnership basis and with less than ten total workers. On the other hand, 'informal workers consist of those working in the informal sector or households, excluding regular workers with social security benefits provided by the employers and workers in the formal sector without any employment and social security benefits provided by the employers' (NCEUS, 2009). According to the estimates provided by the NCEUS, the total employment in the Indian economy was 456 million in 2004-05. Of the total workforce, the informal sector accounted for 86 per cent and the informal workers without any job or social security accounted for 92 per cent. Rural informal workers are mostly poor, unprotected; even their basic needs of food, nutrition, health and employment etc., remain unfulfilled. They have neither regular jobs nor an assured income, so their primary and first need is employment security which is a part of social protection measure. By definition, social protection is broader and more inclusive than social security since it in corporates non-statutory or private measures for providing social security, but still encompasses traditional social security measures such as: social assistance and social insurance. Social protection is defined by the ILO as the set of public measures that a society provides for its members to protect them against economic and social distress that would be caused by the absence or a substantial reduction of income from work as a result of various contingencies (sickness, maternity, employment, injury, unemployment, invalidity, old age, and death of the breadwinner); the provision of health care; and, the provision of benefits for families with children (ILO Report, 1998).

The UPA Government announced the Mahatma Gandhi National Rural Employment Guarantee Act in 2005 to provide employment security to the rural labourers. The main objective of the MGNREGA is 'to enhance livelihood security in rural areas by providing 100 days of guaranteed wage employment in a financial year to every rural household whose adult members volunteer to do unskilled manual work'. However, the performance of the MGNREGS, as revealed by NSS reports and even by government statistics, has been disappointing. According to 66th round NSS report (2009-10), rural households who got work MGNREGA works, worked as an average for 37 days in all over India. Among the Major states, Rajasthan got the maximum number of days of MGNREGA works (71 days), followed by Himachal Pradesh (47 days), Andhra Pradesh (46 days) and Tamil Nadu (43 days). The average number of days of work per household under MGNREGA is lowest in West Bengal (17 days). But the Ministry of Rural Development Report shows slightly higher employment days per household under MGNREGA in West Bengal (22 days) during financial year 2009-10.

Mukherjee and Ghosh (2009) also showed that West Bengal is not among the best performing states in the country in terms of implementation of NREGS. By taking a case study of Birbhum district of West Bengal, they attempt to understand the roles of some macro and micro level factors in determining the success and failures of NREGS implementation. Dey and Bedi (2010) studied the functioning of NREGA between Feb. 2006 and July 2009 in Birbhum district, West Bengal by examining whether the employment guarantee scheme serves as a social safety net by providing a source of source of employment when other alternatives are limited.

No growth assessment study on MGNREGA has been done so far in West Bengal. Against this backdrop, it is important to ask six key questions: *(a)* what is the growth rate of employment generation across districts of West Bengal under MGNREGA? *(b)* Does this growth rate of employment exhibit positive across districts of West Bengal? *(c)* What is the growth rate of expenditure across districts of West Bengal under MGNREGA? *(d)* Does the growth rate of expenditure exhibits positive across districts of West Bengal? *(e)* Is there any linkage between utilisation of funds and availability man days per household under MGNREGA? *(f)* What factors determine the performance of MGNREGA (average man days per household)? To discuss these issues, we rely on data of Ministry of Rural Development for the periods of 2009-10 to 2011-12. We analyse these issues on the basis of five criteria: *(i)* the growth rate of employment generation; *(ii)* the growth rate of average number of days of employment per household; *(iii)* the growth rate of percentage of household completing 100 days of employment under MGNREGA; *(iv)* the growth rate of percentage of expenditure against total available fund and *(v)* the factors determining the performance of MGNREGA (the average man days per household). The paper has three sections. In section 2, we analyse data regarding employment generation, utilisation funds and factors determining the performance of MGNREGA and Section 3 concludes with some policy implication.

II - Employment Generation Under Mgnrega

MGNREGA was implemented in West Bengal in three phases. The first phase was launched in 2006 covering ten most backward districts of West Bengal – South 24 Paraganas, Bankura, Birbhum, Dakshin Dinajpur, Uttar Dinajpur, Jalpaiguri, Malda, West Mednapore, Murshidabad and Purulia. The second phase included seven more districts in 2007 – North 24 Parganas, Burdwan, Coochbehar, Hooghly, Nadia, East Mednapore and Siliguri Mahakuma Parisad (part of Darjeeing district). While Darjeeling Gorkha Hill Council (DGHC) (part of Darjeeling district) and Howrah district were included in 2008. Although the progress of implementation of MGNREGA is not impressive in terms of the number of average person-days of employment generated, the state has succeeded in providing job cards and at least a few days of employment to a large number of households. Up to 2009-10, the total number job cards issued to rural households was 10731321 which increased to 11198268 in 2011-12. But employment provided to households constituted only 46.54 per cent of the total job cards holder households in 2009-10 which has marginally increased to 49.23 per cent in 2011-12. The percentage households getting works out of total job cards holders in MGNREGA works varied from 20 per cent of the job cards holder households in Uttar Dinajpur district to 74.08 per cent in Burdwan district during 2011-12 (Table 5.1). The households getting MGNREGA works is low among job cards holders of first phase backwards districts as compared to second and third phase districts. Out of 18 districts, only in five districts (namely: Burdwan, Coochbehar, Hooghly, Darjeeling and Howrah), percentage household getting works under MGNREGA increased continuously during 2009-10 to 2011-12. The low percentage of households getting in MGNREGA works raised question about usefulness of MGNREGA in these districts. Do these households receive better wages or better work opportunities in other sectors rather than MGNREGA works? The main reason of low percentage of households getting MGNREGA works in spite of having their job cards are the lack of awareness, lack of proper information regarding employment availability, low level of utilisation of fund and availability of work during busy agricultural seasons.

The percentage of household getting MGNAREGA works out of total job cards holder households is low (less than 50%) in West Bengal and efforts should be taken to provide MGNAREGA works to more rural households to solve the problems of unemployment and under-employment in rural areas. We have calculated annual compound growth rate of household getting MGNREGA works in rural areas. The annual compound growth rate of households getting MGNAREGA is only 3.35 per cent during 2009-10 to 2011-12 (Table 5.1). Some first phase districts (namely: Daksin Dinajpur, Jalpaiguri and Murshidabad) exhibit the negative growth rate of households getting MGNAREGA works during this period. Second phase two districts (namely: Uttar 24 Parganas and Nadia) exhibits the negative growth of households getting MGNAREGA works. Darjeeling district is recorded the highest growth rate of households getting MGNAREGA works out of total job cards holder households..

In West Bengal, the increase in the average number of person-days of employment from 22 days in 2009-10 to 27 days in 2011-12 has been possible due to better performances of some districts mainly three first phase districts (South 24 Parganas, Bankura and Birbhum);

Table 5.1: Trends of Percentage of Households Getting Works under MGNREGA out of Total Job Cards Holder Households and Annual Compound Growth Rate of Households Getting MGNREGA Works across Districts of West Bengal

	Districts	2009-10	2010-11	2011-12	Annual Compound Growth Rate of Households Getting MGNREGA during 2009-10 to 2011-12
1.	South 24 Parganas	18.07	14.04	24.38	12.29
2.	Bankura	36.83	57.34	56.56	17.42
3.	Birbhum	71.75	69.80	71.29	.53
4.	Dakshin Dinajpur	33.16	26.29	26.98	-5.28
5.	Uttar Dinajpur	11.20	21.85	20.62	23.09
6.	Jalpaiguri	68.08	63.40	62.10	-2.32
7.	Maldah	30.92	22.27	32.99	2.97
8.	West Mednapore	59.19	60.94	59.76	1.96
9.	Murshidabad	43.91	46.98	38.67	-2.95
10.	Pululia	43.61	47.48	42.86	.17
11.	North 24 Parganas	50.38	46.78	45.81	-1.35
12.	Burdwan	68.69	71.88	74.08	4.52
13.	Coochbehar	45.46	47.65	48.87	3.16
14.	Hooghly	49.58	62.42	67.82	14.16
15.	Nadia	52.00	42.81	37.74	9.56
16	East Mednapore	47.83	44.59	51.11	3.96
17.	Darjeeling	16.79	45.45	63.43	64.34
18.	Howrah	23.84	27.11	32.87	13.23
19.	Total	46.53	47.93	49.23	3.35

Source: Calculated from data provided on www.nregs.nic.in

two second phase districts (North 24 Parganas and Hooghly) and Darjeeling district (third phase) (Table 5.2). Among the first phase districts, the lowest numbers of person days were generated in Uttar Dinajpur district in all three years. Dakshin Dianjpur and Murshidabad which are also first phase districts and backwards in terms of human development indicators, has failed to show any noticeable progress in

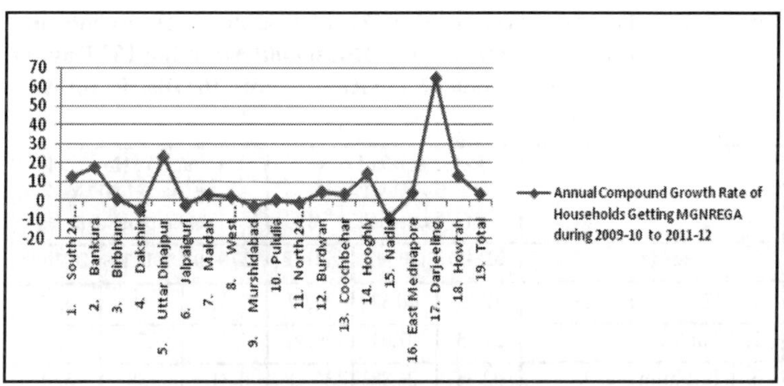

Fig. 5.1: **Annual Compound Growth Rate of Households Getting MGNREGA during 2009-10 to 2011-12**

generating employment for rural poor. In the second phase districts too, the performance of MGNREGA is ordinary. Only about 26 person-days were generated per household during 2011-12 in these districts with little variation among them. The creation of an average number of person-days of employment per household is the lowest in the Coochbehar and the highest in Nort 24 Parganas, among these districts. In the third phase, Darjeeling district is recorded highest (50 days per household) for generating employment days per household. However, across the districts, the value of standard deviation also increased over the periods. An important point to be noted here is that the percentage of MGNREGA households completing 100 days of work is still very low in West Bengal (only 2.16% in 2011-12) (Table 5.2). It varies from 18 per cent in Coochbehar district to 5.81 per cent in Birbhum district in 2011-12. However, in 12 out of the total of 18 districts, the percentage has shown an increase between 2009-10 and 2011-12. But the value of standard deviation fluctuates during these periods and the value of standard deviation in 2011-12 is lower than the year 2010-11. If the level of participation by working households, the average number of days of MGNREGA work, and percentage of households completing 100 days is assessed, one can say that the potential of MGNREGA is still far from fully tapped (Hirway, 2010).

The employment days available per household in West Bengal is comparatively low as compared to other states. To fulfill the target of 100 days of employment per household, growth rate of

Table 5.2: Trends of Average Man Days Available per Houschold and Trends of Percentage of Household Attaining 100 Days of Employment under MGNREGA Across the Districts of West Bengal

		Average Man Days Available Per Houschold			Percentage of Household Attaining 100 Days of Employment		
	Districts	2009-10	2010-11	2011-12	2009-10	2010-11	2011-12
1.	South 24 Parganas	17.16	20.32	32.09	.64	.93	3.74
2.	Bankura	22.63	37.64	30.56	1.49	7.73	3.89
3.	Birbhum	22.38	26.38	36.14	1.31	2.38	5.81
4.	Dakshin Dinajpur	19.18	20.33	21.16	.81	1.02	1.32
5.	Uttar Dinajpur	11.56	17.04	18.36	.06	.64	.87
6.	Jalpaiguri	25.49	23.20	25.88	.59	.87	1.13
7.	Maldah	18.67	22.34	28.94	.45	1.44	2.59
8.	West Mednapore	26.77	29.87	24.73	1.98	2.58	1.23
9.	Murshidabad	18.85	24.80	21.92	.84	1.78	1.04
10.	Pululia	26.75	33.47	28.68	3.83	5.35	3.48
11.	North 24 Parganas	28.31	32.22	34.43	1.63	2.77	2.81
12.	Burdwan	24.40	32.79	25.25	1.92	4.37	1.11
13.	Coochbehar	13.74	13.98	14.10	.07	.17	.18
14.	Hooghly	17.18	28.68	30.73	1.00	2.23	2.09
15.	Nadia	19.83	19.16	19.06	.46	.57	.64
16.	East Mednapore	23.35	23.63	26.70	1.17	1.17	1.60
17.	Darjeeling	15.24	31.18	40.66	.31	4.06	5.54
18.	Howrah	12.48	16.31	19.81	.27	.50	.83
19.	Total	21.96	26.97	27.07	1.23	2.57	2.16
	Standard Deviation	5.00	6.52	6.55	.89	2.11	1.62

Source: Calculated from data provided on www.nregs.nic.in

employment generation under MGNAREGA should be increased in West Bengal. We have estimated annual compound growth rate of person-days generation under MGNAREGA across districts of West Bengal for the periods 2009-10 to 2011-12 (Table 5.3). The annual compound growth rate of person-days generation under MGNAREGA in West Bengal is only 10.81 per cent during this period. Some first phase districts (namely: West Mednapore, Jalpaiguri and Dakshin

Dinajpur) exhibit the negative annual compound growth rate of person-days generation during this reference periods. In the case of second phase districts, only one district (Nadia) exhibits negative growth of person-days generation under MGNAREGA. Darjeeling district is recorded the highest growth rate of person-days generation under MGNAREGA followed by Uttar Dinajpur District and Hooghly district.

Table 5.3: Annual Compound Growth Rate of Employment Generation and Expenditure, and Trend of Percentage of Utilisation of Funds under MGNREGA Across Districts of West Bengal

		Annual Compound Growth Rate of Employment Generation	Annual Compound Growth Rate of Expenditure	Trends of Percentage of Utilization of Funds		
	Districts	Annual Compound Growth Rate of Employment Generation during 2009-10 to 2011-12	Annual Compound Growth Rate of Expenditure during 2009-10 to 2011-12	2009-10	2010-11	2011-12
1.	South 24 Parganas	38.34	34.40	77.81	64.64	86.79
2.	Bankura	29.79	14.96	85.29	80.30	91.98
3.	Birbhum	17.95	17.37	91.92	89.78	93.60
4.	Dakshin Dinajpur	-2.11	-6.32	76.40	73.17	85.82
5.	Uttar Dinajpur	43.67	6.84	92.09	70.93	82.78
6.	Jalpaiguri	-1.77	-2.30	93.52	87.58	90.56
7.	Maldah	19.16	15.51	87.50	96.61	96.09
8.	West Mednapore	-.69	17.48	89.05	70.56	82.99
9.	Murshidabad	2.05	4.65	88.78	74.26	93.97
10.	Pululia	2.52	-20.65	94.24	73.82	91.80
11.	North 24 Parganas	5.29	12.04	94.24	93.02	94.33
12.	Burdwan	7.40	9.64	98.96	84.48	91.82
13.	Coochbehar	4.05	-2.65	80.30	79.01	79.79
14.	Hooghly	38.58	24.04	89.90	88.59	93.02
15.	Nadia	-9.97	5.71	94.73	78.82	96.99
16.	East Mednapore	8.70	16.62	91.49	87.32	95.86
17.	Darjeeling	127.95	67.02	75.04	73.23	94.00
18.	Howrah	32.08	32.47	758.33	76.37	80.06
19.	Total	10.81	10.33	90.71	81.57	91.22

Source: Calculated from data provided on www.nregs.nic.in

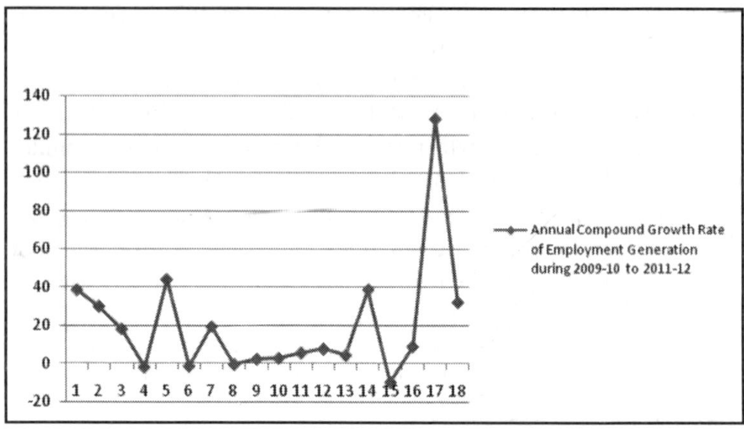

Fig. 5.2: **Annual Compound Growth Rate of Employment Generation during 2009-10 to 2011-12**

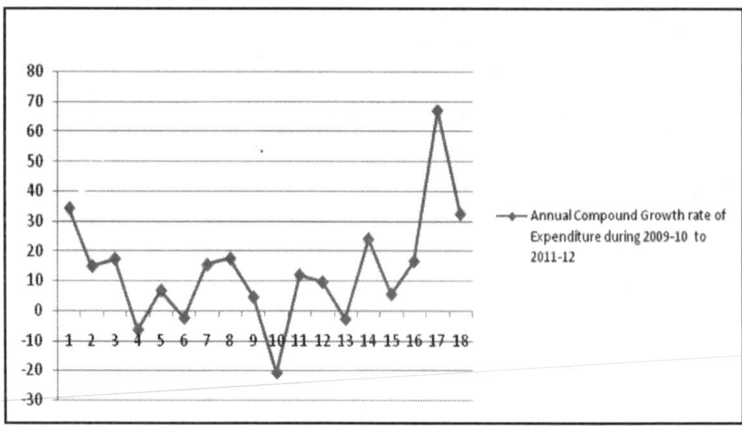

Fig. 5.3: **Annual Compound Growth rate of Expenditure during 2009-10 to 2011-12**

A similar inter-district difference was found in the case of utilization of MGNREGA fund. The utilisation of fund across districts varied 80 per cent to 90 per cent of the available fund under MGNREGA during 2011-12 (Table 5.3). Out of 18 districts, 12 districts could spend more than 90 per cent of the available fund under MGNREGA during 2011-12. Is there any positive relation between the utilisation of the available MGNREGA funds and the average number of person-days per household at the district level? On other words, had the districts which spent most of the available funds under MGNREGA succeeded in creating a higher number of average person-days? From the table, we did not get any clear relation between the utilisation of available funds and average number of person-days created. However, districts which has utilised 90 per cent or more of the available funds exhibit negative relationship (Pearson correlation coefficient = -0.18). On the other hand, districts which has utilised 80 per cent but less than 90 per cent of the available funds exhibit positive relationship (Pearson correlation co-efficient = 0.74). It is clear that a district may exhaust all its funds and still be unable to generate an average number of person-days close to 100 days. These findings indicate that hardly any district was able to come up with an adequate number of schemes to absorb all households demanding works under MGNREGA.

Expenditure incurred by districts in West Bengal for generating MGNREGA works is not adequate to ensure 100 days of employment per household. Funds of MGNREGA have been sanctioned on the basis of plan proposals submitted by PRI. The capacity of PRI becomes crucial factor for successful implementation of the programme. The capacity of the PRI indicates both physical capacity (*i.e.,* more technical and skilled manpower) as well as the capacity to produce meaningful plans in sufficient numbers so that those who demand work can be provided employment. The capacity of PRI to spend more funds under MGNREGA should be increased many folds to ensure 100 days of employment per household in the rural areas. The annual compound growth of expenditure under MGNREGA in West Bengal is only 10.33 per cent during 2009-10 to 2011-12 and there is also inter districts variation in the growth rate of expenditure under MGNREGA (Table 5.3). The first phase of some districts (namely: Dakshin Dinajpur, Jalpaiguri and Purulia) and second phase one district (namely Coochbehar) exhibit negative growth of expenditure during this period. Darjeeling district is recorded the highest growth of expenditure under MGNREGA but even failed to ensure 100 days of employment per household for the rural people who demanded works under MGNREGA.

Factors Affecting Performance of MGNREGA

The performance of MGNREGA *i.e.,* average man days per households depend certain variables *i.e.*, awareness level of the labour households, cropping intensity and per cent of SC and ST population of the total population in a district. Literacy Rate is used here as a proxy for the awareness level of the labour households. It is expected that the awareness level of labourers is positively correlated with the average man days per household. Cropping intensity is an indicator of agricultural development of a region. High cropping Intensity implies agriculturally developed region which can provide more employment days to the labourers and reduce the dependency on employment under MGNREGA. So the cropping intensity of a district negatively influenced the average man days per household. It is expected that the scheduled caste and scheduled tribe concentrated region need more employment under MGNREGA. So the more average man days per household should be ensured for the scheduled caste and scheduled tribe concentrated regions.

OLS technique is used for identifying the determinants of performance of the MGNREGA (average man days per household). The estimated model is given as follows:

AD = f (LR, CI, PP).

Where

AD = Average man days per household.

CI = Cropping Intensity.

LR = Literacy Rate.

PP = Percentage of Scheduled Caste and Scheduled Tribe population.

From Table 5.4, it is clear that variables like: literacy rate, cropping intensity and concentration of scheduled caste and scheduled tribe population in a particular region influenced the performance of MGNREGA (average man days per household) significantly. Moreover, all the estimated co-efficients are statistically significant. The high literacy rate of a district implies high awareness level of the labour households regarding MGNREGA resulted high average man days per household in this district. The better performance districts include: North 24 Parganas, South 24 Parganas, Bankura, Birbhum and Darjeeling whose average man day per household is 30 man days or more during 2011-12. On the other hand, the least performance districts like: Uttar Dinajpur, Dakshin Dinajpur, Coochbehar, Murshidabad, Nadia and Howrah, their average man days per household is around 22 man days or less. The literacy rate of the better performance districts is high as compared to the least performance district. The cropping intensity of better performance districts is low as compared to the least performance districts. Low cropping intensity of a particular district increases the dependency on employment of MGNREGA. It is expected that the performance of Scheduled caste and Scheduled tribe concentrated district will be better but it is not happened. The concentration of Scheduled caste and scheduled tribe population negatively influenced the performance of MGNREGA.

Table 5.4: Determinants of Performance of MGNREGA Across Districts of West Bengal

	Districts	Literacy Rate	Cropping Intensity	% of SC and ST Population
20.	South 24 Parganas	76.78	134	33.35
21.	Bankura	69.60	136	41.60
22.	Birbhum	69.25	166	36.25
23.	DakshinDinajpur	71.18	165	44.90
24.	Uttar Dinajpur	57.15	186	32.82
25.	Jalpaiguri	70.55	166	55.58
26.	Maldah	60.42	201	23.74
27.	West Mednapore	77.92	167	48.31
28.	Murshidabad	66.27	237	13.29
29.	Pululia	63.75	107	36.56
30.	North 24 Parganas	78.11	178	22.83
31.	Burdwan	73.39	183	33.39
32.	Coochbehar	73.87	194	50.68
33.	Hooghly	79.22	237	27.79
34.	Nadia	71.50	253	32.14
35.	East Mednapore	87.47	173	46.50
36.	Darjeeling	74.97	122	28.78
37.	Howrah	80.82	215	15.86
38.	Total			

Source: Economic Review (2011-12), West Bengal.

Conclusion and Suggestions

The performance of West Bengal in terms of generating the number of average days of MGNREGA works per household is not comparable to that of best performing states in the country. The percentage of households completing 100 days of works is highly insignificant. There is no record of providing unemployment benefits to the concerned households who were not provided employment demanded by them within stipulated time frame. Wages are also not paid within time, that is, within 15 days of completion of the work. The performance of MGNREGA (average man days per household) depends certain factors like awareness level of the labour households, cropping intensity and per cent of SC and ST population of the total population in a district. PRI is the main agency to implement the MGNREGA but the poor ability of PRI to play their role is a major factor behind the poor performance of MGNREGA in West Bengal. GPS are not equipped with required staff for planning and implementing MGNREGA works. They also lack the required technical and administrative support as well as funds in their hands to carry out MGNREGA works efficiently. Thus, in order to facilitate the planning process and proper implementation of MGNREGA by GPs, comprehensive training on various issues during the process of implementation is utmost importance. Training on various aspects such as: maintenance of records and registrars, administrative procedures involved at the GP level, grievance handling mechanisms, process of conducting social audit, and awareness generation at the village level about the entitlements of MGNREGA, are important.

Table 5.5: Estimates of Determinants of Performance of MGNREGA in West Bengal

Variables	Co-efficient	T-Value
Constant	42.475	2.88**
Literacy Rate	.224	1.25*
Cropping Intensity	-.124	-3.44***
% of SC and ST Population	-.283	-2.28**

Sample Size = 18

Adjusted R Square = .38

*, ** and *** indicate significant at 10%, 5% and 1% level respectively.

Recent policies of the National Democratic Alliance (NDA) Government at the centre regarding MGNREGA have created an impression among the public that the Government is inimical to the implementation of this employment generation programme. According to the information accessed by activists using RTI, a note written by the Secretary (Rural Development), Government of India in August 2014 stated, 'In my considered opinion, the programme needs better targeting. MGNREGA 2005 does not require all Indian coverage. The Act needs to be amended through the Parliament to enable its coverage only in backward districts/blocks'. The Minister of rural Development also accepted this suggestion of better targeting MGNREGA to backwards blocks. From these notes at least intentions and views at the highest level are evident that the 'national' character of the path breaking rural employment guarantee legislation should be changed and MGNREGA should be confined to only some districts/ classified as 'backwards' (The Statesman, October, 2014). Another expected chance is to change the labour material expense ratio in MGNREGA works from 60:40 to 51:49. This change was supported by the Minster of Rural development in the Parliament debate on MGNREGA on July, 2014. However, in a note of August, 2014, a Joint Secretary, Rural development pointed out that several problems associated with such a change. This note says, 'The proposal to change this ratio to 51:49 and make it applicable at the district level, though is legally and technically possible, runs contrary to the spirit of the Act which has been made for creating employment opportunities for the unskilled workers who face considerable vulnerabilities during lean agricultural season' (The Statesman, October, 2014).

The reduction in budgetary allocation for MGNREGA has been started since UPA II Government by cutting down funds from Rs. 40,000 crore in the budgets of 2010-11 and 2011-12 to Rs. 33,000 crore in the subsequent two budgets. Moreover, the present Government at the Centre has virtually capped the expenditure refusing legitimate demands of the states for more allocation on the basis of demand for work by the rural people where as the previous Government kept it open-ended with a proviso to meet the additional demands of the states as per requirement. Given that the basis of the legal guarantee of 100 days of work is demand driven, imposing such a cap is clearly a violation of the law (The Hindu, October, 2014). Another important thing is that the increase in the ratio of materials will automatically mean the entry of contractors and machines in much large numbers into the MGNREGA projects. This in turn will signify the conversion of MGNREGA from a work guarantee act into a contractor's commission guarantee act (The Hindu, October, 2014).

So the demand driver character of MGNREGA should be maintained and work seekers should be provided work on demand as it is a legal guarantee of work. But previously, in order to universalize this programme in a rush, quality of works have not been maintained and also got incentives for proliferation of corruption practices. For example, there are countless instances of labour – scarce in the country, where the pressure to spend under MGNREGA led to contractors, in collusion with bureaucrats, deploying machines for doing the work and fudging entries in job-cards of workers who sat at home and pocketed part of wages (The Hindu, November, 2014). In case of West Bengal, it was also found the eagerness of bureaucrats to universalize the programme by creating pressure at lower level to spend more money which increased corruption practices and deteriorated quality of works under MGNREGA. To avoid such situations, it is imperative that the demand driven character of MGNREGA be deeply respected. Awareness among workers should be increased regarding their entitlements as envisaged in the National rural Employment Guarantee Act (MGNREGA), so that they can demand for job under MGNREGA. Even now MGNREGA is supply driven in nature. In such a situation, the proposal regarding restricting MGNREGA to certain selected and short-listed regions where the need for such job-guarantee projects are needed more and have called it a death knell for the scheme. Instead of restricting the implementation of MGNREGA in certain regions, flow of funds should be made available for all regions as per demand for the successful implementation of this job guarantee programme.

It was expected that the adoption of new economic policy will lead to higher growth rates, job creation, and hence decreased to poverty and more equitable distribution of incomes in the country. But actually, high growth rates did not necessarily lead to reduction of poverty and inequality of income, as experienced in the Latin American Countries, South Asian countries. So the country needs such structural transformation and growth rates which will absorb unemployed and under employed labour force of the economy. In such a situation, the Government acting as an employer of the last resort (ELR) and thus implementing a public employment guarantee policy (EGP) can go a long way. ELR and EGP ought to be considered as an instrumental part of the policy mix that shields the people against unemployment and inactivity (Raina, 2007). The idea of Government as employer of last resort is not a novel one. Such initiatives can be traced back centuries

– for example, to the fourteenth century, when Mohammad Bin Tughlaq, ruler of India, sought to create work projects to avert famine (Drez and Sen, 1989). Often credited to J.M. Keynes, during the past century there has been recognition that underemployment and forced 'inactivity' are integral parts of market systems. Unless full employment is a key economic objective, there is no known automatic internal mechanism that creates jobs in numbers that match the number of people willing, able, and ready to work. Here in lies the rationale of the government as an employer of the last resort (Minsky, 1965, 1986).

REFERENCES

1. Dey, Subhasis and Bedi, Arjun (2010). 'The National Rural Employment Guarantee Scheme in Birbhum', *Economic and Political Weekly*, Vol. XLV, No. 41.
2. Dogra, Bharat (2014). 'MGNREGA Set For Drastic Overhaul', The Statesman, October, 27.
3. Hirway, Indira (2010). 'NREGA After Four Years: Building on Experiences to Move Ahead', *The Indian Journal of Labour Economics*', Vol. 53, No. 1.
4. ILO (1998). 'Decent Work', Report of the Director-General, Geneva. www.ilo.org/public/english/standards/ relm/ilc/ilc87/rep-i.htm.
5. Jha, Raghbendra and Gaiha, Raghav (2012). 'NREGS: Interpreting the Official Statistics', *Economic and Political Weekly*, Vol. XLVII, No. 40.
6. Karat, Brinda (2014). 'Ending Destitution and Distress', The Hindu, October, 25.
7. Mohan, Sumitra (2014). 'Truncated NREGS', The Statesman, December, 27.
8. Mukherjee, Subrata and Ghosh, Saswata (2009). 'What Determines The Success of NREGS at the Panchayat Level? – A Case Study of Birbhum Districtin west Bengal', *The Indian Journal of Labour Economics*, Vol. 52, No. 1.
9. National Sample Survey Organization (NSSO) (2011). 'Employment and Unemployment Situation in India, 2009-10: NSSO 66th Round (Report No. 537), Ministry of Statistics and Programme Implementation, Government of India, New Delhi.
10. NCEUS (2007). 'Report on Conditions of Work and Promotion of Livelihood in the Unorganized Sector', National Commission for Enterprises in the Unorganized Sector, Government of India, New Delhi.
11. NCEUS, Government of India (2009). 'The Challenge of Employment in India – An Informal Economy Perspective', Academic foundation New Delhi.
12. Saini, Debi S. (2007). 'Securing Working Class Rights for Informal Sector Workers in India: A Case Study of Self-Employed Women's Association', The Indian Journal of Labour Economics, Vol. 50, No. 4.
13. Shah, Mihir (2014), 'How to reform and How Not To', The Hindu, November, 4.

Pages: 104-114

Rural Economy: ***Changing Landscape***

Edited by: **Dr. Kartick Das**

ISBN: 978-93-5056-838-5

Edition: **2017**

Published by: **Discovery Publishing House Pvt. Ltd., New Delhi (India)**

Impact of Micro-Plot Allocation Programme in Addressing Poverty and Landlessness

A Case Study of West Bengal

— **Sudipta Biswas**

INTRODUCTION

India is the home for about one third of the extreme poor people in the world (MDG Report, 2014). In rural India an estimated 15 million extremely poor families are landless (RDI, 2009). A World Bank study shows that landlessness is the greatest predictor of poverty in India, finding the incidence of poverty to be 68 per cent among landless wage earners. By comparison, the incidence of poverty was found to be 51 per cent for Scheduled Caste (SC), Scheduled Tribes (ST); and 45 per cent for households where no one was literate. The government has recently released Socio-economic Caste Census, 2011 report and considered landlessness as a major indicator of rural poverty perhaps for the first time. The figures indicate that almost 54 per cent of the rural population lives without any ownership of land. On the other hand, India Rural Development Report 2012-2013, released by Infrastructure Development Finance Corporation shows that nearly half of all Indians still depend on land and land-based activities for their livelihoods. The fact of dependence of half of Indian population on land and land based livelihood while 54 per cent of them without access to land is definitely a matter of grave concern for policy-makers and thinker.

Most Indian states enacted land reform laws aimed at broadening access to rural land. These land reform laws have by and large enabled redistribution of ceiling surplus land and regulation or prohibition of landlord-tenant relationship. But, studies show that these efforts have very marginal impact in broadening access to rural land. Even in most successful states like: West Bengal, Kerala and Karnataka the problem of rural landlessness remained substantial mostly because of lack of political will to implement these traditional means of land reforms.

Role of Micro-Plots in Addressing Rural Landlessness

Different international experiences and field studies have offered solution to address the issues of rural landlessness through an innovative approach; distribution of micro-plots among rural landless households even at the cost of purchasing land from the market by the government. When rural families have secure access to and control over land, they are likely to grow more food and see their incomes rise. Land security for the rural poor families can mean food security as well as social security. Empirical evidences suggest that once women have more control over land, this would give them more power in the community and reduce their vulnerability within their household. Studies have proved that a rural household can get multiple benefits – food, income, status and economic security, from a very small parcel of land, particularly when the plots are large enough to include a garden and a space for a few animals (optimum size being 5-15 cent). Homestead plots enhance family income and economic security as they can produce a surplus for sale in the market and provide something for the family to fall back on in times of need. Ownership of micro-plot helps enhance status and self-image of rural households. It helps access credit and enables a family to enjoy other rights and entitlements. Thus, allocation of homestead plots can be used as a critical tool to providing the rural poor with access to land.

Findings of a research study conducted by Rural Development Institute (Landesa), USA and University of Agricultural Science, Bangalore in 2001 regarding significant benefits yielded from micro-plots are worth mentioning here.

- Functionally landless, agricultural labourer families that own a house plot typically derive substantial non-housing benefits from the plot including: increased nutrition, income, status, wealth generation, and access to credit.
- Those benefits increase very substantially with relatively small increases in house plot size, especially as the house plot increases above 3 cents.

- Families with house plots larger than 3 cents were more than twice as likely as those with smaller plots to report that the plot had resulted in improved nutrition; and almost twice as likely to report that receiving the plot had increased their access to credit.
- Rural families with well-developed house-and – garden plots of about 7 cent were producing enough vegetables, fruits, and milk on their homestead plots to meet or significantly exceed their household nutritional needs of these products. Apart from direct household consumption, these households received about Rs. 11,000 of annualized income from the sale of products from their house-and-garden plots.

Efforts by some States through Micro-Plots Allocation Programmes

Some state government included allocation of micro-plots to rural landless households as post-independence land reform agenda. States have distributed land from a variety of sources, including: vested ceiling surplus land, state government land and land under the control of local governments. Some land distribution programmes do not provide new land but grant current occupants enhanced rights like granting residential tenant ownership of the land they occupy, regularizing the possession of illegally occupied land etc. Some states like: West Bengal and Bihar enacted separate laws for one or more of these methods but most states have incorporated provisions in their land reform laws, land revenue laws, or both. Kerala government run homestead plot allocation programme during 1970s-1980s and 2,84,203 families acquired permanent rights to their homesteads (P.S. Appu: 1996).

Later on, several state government initiated homestead plot allocation programmes which varies across states in terms of size of land, mode of implementation etc., the basic objective remaining the same. Namma Bhumi-Namma Thota (My Land My Garden) in Karnataka, Cultivation and Dwelling Plots Allotment Scheme (CDPA) in West Bengal, Land Purchase Project Subcomponent under Indira Kranthi Patham (IKP) in Andhra Pradesh and Vasundhara in Odisha are worth mentioning here. Pursuant to these laws and provisions, an estimated four million households received homestead plots across India till 2007. The plots typically have ranged in size from 0.02 acre to 0.1 acre (Tim Hanstad, T. Haque, Robin Nielsen; 2008).

West Bengal and its Micro-Plots Allocation Programme

The State Scenario

West Bengal is the second most densely populated state and it has the third largest number of poor people in India with a total of 52.2 million living in poverty according to the Multidimensional Poverty Index developed by the Oxford University. The service industry in the state has experienced substantial growth but agriculture remains to be the main occupation in the state. West Bengal ranked 9th among 15 major states in India in terms of Human Poverty Index (HPI) measured by using National Family Health Survey-3 data for the year 2005-06. Deprivation of public provisioning has been very high compared to health deprivation and deprivation in knowledge. There has been secular decline in rural poverty in West Bengal during the last two decades. The Headcount Ratio (HCR) of rural poverty shows a declining trend from 73.16 per cent in 1973-74 to 40.8 per cent in 1993-94, 31.85 per cent in 1999-2000, and further to 28.6 per cent in 2004-05 (West Bengal State Development Report, 2008).

Landlessness in the State and Introduction of Micro-Plot Allocation Programme

The State is widely recognised as one of the most progressive states in redistributive land reform. West Bengal was also at the forefront among states in terms of effective distribution of ceiling-surplus land, having allocated 1.04 million acres of land to 2.54 million land-poor households by 2001 (Hanstad and Brown, 2001). In spite of its noteworthy attempts to reduce the land-poverty, West Bengal is the home for a large number of rural landless families. As per National Sample Survey Organization (NSSO) 66th round data (2009-10), there are around 0.55 million landless poor families in rural West Bengal. But, as per an estimate by the government of West Bengal, the number of rural landless families in the state was around 0.35 million. The Government of West Bengal launched Cultivation and Dwelling Plot Allotment (CDPA) Scheme, the homestead plot allocation programme in 2006 to provide land for the poorest landless and homesteadless agricultural labourer households. The programme had the provision of allocation of 10-16 decimal of land to rural landless agricultural labourers. Till October, 2011, the state government has provided micro-plots to 6954 rural households for making dwelling units and utilising rest of the land for production purposes. The programme was amended in 2009 after conducting field studies followed by certain recommendations by Landesa.

Introduction of Nijo Griha Nijo Bhumi (NGNB)

Later on, when new government came into power they renamed the programme as Nijo Griha, Nijo Bhumi (My Home My Land) or NGNB in 2011 with certain changes in the provisions of CDPA. The NGNB programme is mainly implemented by the Department of Land and Land Reforms, with major roles for the Block Development Office and Panchayati Raj Institutions (PRIs). As per the provision of the programme, government purchases land suitable for homestead development at the market price to be distributed to landless labourers, artisans and fishermen for settling them in a cluster of minimum ten families. In addition to the allotment of purchased land, there is also provision for distribution of ceiling surplus vested vacant land or regularization of encroached government vested land. The programme has recently expanded its scope of purchasing *'rayati'* land from private owners which are already occupied by landless families.

NGNB and its Role in Addressing Landlessness

Under the programme, an eligible family is provided with maximum 5 decimal of land for making dwelling units and utilising rest of the land for livelihood augmentation. Women headed households from Scheduled Tribes (STs) are given first priority, women headed households from Scheduled Castes (SC), then minority communities, and finally those belonging to any other caste. Next priority is given to male-headed households in the same order with titles in joint names of wife and husband. There is a programme implementation committee at the block level, called Land Purchase and Land Distribution (LPLD) Committee to ensure certain quality aspect of land distribution. After selection of the households in order of priority, suitable land is identified, purchased and allocated to those families. Government provides support for relocation of those families in a cluster by providing basic infrastructure support through convergence with existing other government schemes and programmes. Under the convergence component of the programme, the government provides agricultural extension services for livelihood development by leveraging support from government resources.

Table 6.1: Progress of Micro-Plot Distribution since inception to March 2015

District	Number of Families Benefitted During									Total Number of Families Benefitted under CDPA, NGNB and Sec. 49(1)			
	Apr. 2006-Oct. 2011	November 2011–March 2012		2012-13		2013-14		2014-15					
	CDPA	NGNB	Agri. patta u/s 49 (1)	NGNB	Agri. patta u/s 49 (1)	NGNB	Agri. patta u/s 49 (1)	NGNB	Agri. patta u/s 49 (1)	CDPA	NGNB	Agri. patta u/s 49 (1)	Grand Total
Bankura	671	0	305	3552	1211	2221	261	286	0	671	6059	1777	8507
Barddhaman	154	1164	1527	6503	4293	7866	134	7815	0	154	23348	5954	29456
Birbhum	171	0	903	5206	428	9139	106	625	0	171	14970	1437	16578
Hooghly	24	59	2443	847	1150	3604	86	732	0	24	5242	3679	8945
Paschim Medinipur	1345	211	1929	5392	2727	8191	1619	2311	91	1345	16105	6366	23816
Purba Medinipur	438	5	1554	3017	3360	5250	0	248	212	438	8520	5126	14084
Purulia	144	188	387	1569	1858	4757	999	612	0	144	7126	3244	10514
Haora	275	16	101	516	193	774	134	2259	0	275	3565	428	4268
Nadia	125	0	637	3107	3344	14105	373	1482	0	125	18694	4354	23173
Murshidabad	81	92	1850	4076	944	3869	45	177	0	81	8214	2839	11134
North 24 Parganas	297	75	1252	2254	1611	2011	1	0	0	297	4340	2864	7501

Contd...

District	Number of Families Benefitted During									Total Number of Families Benefitted under CDPA, NGNB and Sec. 49(1)			
	Apr. 2006-Oct. 2011	November 2011 – March 2012		2012-13		2013-14		2014-15					
	CDPA	NGNB	Agri. patta u/s 49 (1)	NGNB	Agri. patta u/s 49 (1)	NGNB	Agri. patta u/s 49 (1)	NGNB	Agri. patta u/s 49 (1)	CDPA	NGNB	Agri. patta u/s 49 (1)	Grand Total
South 24 Parganas	199	918	1189	10047	6003	10750	133	3069	0	199	24784	7325	32308
Jalpaiguri	294	48	1412	6319	5978	7012	0	2009	0	294	15388	7390	23072
Alipurduar (created on 25th June 2014)	0	0	0	0	0	0	0	271	60	0	271	60	331
Darjeeling	1048	0	323	1503	0	3493	0	3786	0	1048	8782	323	10153
Coochbehar	819	0	691	2178	1055	5161	82	1677	0	819	9016	1828	11663
Malda	442	237	1618	2148	712	3780	143	3756	0	442	9921	2473	12836
Uttar Dinajpur	100	27	616	2689	1315	5678	325	692	12	100	9086	2268	11454
Dakhin Dinajpur	327	0	336	1244	279	2757	718	585	0	327	4586	1333	6246
Total	6954	3040	19073	62167	36461	100418	5159	32392	375	6954	198017	61068	266039

Source: Directorate of Land Records and Survey. Department of Land and Land Reforms, Government of West Bengal.

It is noteworthy to mention that apart from the aforesaid NGNB programme, the government is still providing '*patta*' (land titles) to land poor families for agriculture purposes under Section 49 (1) of the West Bengal Land Reforms Act, 1955. The state government conducted another survey in the year 2013 and it was found that the number of landless poor families have come down considerably. An estimated 0.22 million rural households still remained landless (Department of Land and Land Reforms, Government of West Bengal). Till 31st March 2015, the government has been able to secure homestead plots to 2,66,039 rural households. District wise performance of the micro-plot allocation programme is shown in Table 6.1.

Since the West Bengal is densely populated there is huge land crunch in the state. Considering this reality, though CDPA Programme has not been able to address rural landlessness in terms of quantity but, it has helped beneficiary families to ensure rise in level of income, food security in the family and empowering them. On the other hand, NGNB Programme has been able to cover huge number of landless families including regularization of occupants of government vested lands. It has instilled confidence among landless families by rooting out fear of eviction, thus ensuring secured tenure. NGNB Programme has played crucial role in addressing tribal landlessness spread across West Midnapore, Purulia, Bankura, Jalpaiguri and Bardhhaman districts. Apart from that, a huge number of Scheduled Caste families, landlessness among them being the matter of concern, have been covered by the programme. Above all, in 95 per cent cases women's name in the land titles either singly or jointly has been ensured by the programme which can be considered as major success in addressing gender dimension of the issue.

Outcomes of the Micro-Plot Allocation Programme

As a measure of post-land allocation convergence support, enshrined in the NGNB Programme implementation guideline, micro-plot recipient families have received support for land development, development of internal roads, drinking water support, electricity connection etc., in at least 60 per cent places where families have been settled in purchased land in the form of a cluster. Field evidences also reflect that around 30 per cent regularized families have received at least 1-2 convergence supports. Getting land titles in the hand enabled those families for the entitlement of other government supports like:

housing, toilets, institutional credits, livestock supports etc. Landesa working in partnership with the state government has been promoting site specific convergence model and facilitating convergence support in particular sites by leveraging support from other government schemes and programmes. The organization has also been facilitating the government to replicate the model in a scalable manner in other potential places. The organization is also promoting agricultural extension support to specific sites for livelihood augmentation of micro-plot recipient families. There are many examples where beneficiary families have received training and other inputs from the government and started income generating activities to come out of poverty. Though comprehensive data is not available to evaluate the impact of the programme as a whole, but evidences and case stories available from the fields are enough to substantiate the fact.

Impact of the Programme

The programme has brought about certain qualitative changes in the lives of the poor landless families. Field evidences show that a piece of land has enhanced confidence and self-esteem to take planned steps towards a life with dignity and prosperity. It has diversified livelihood options and enhanced income of those families. There is a security that the families are staying at their own land. Micro-plot recipient families reported that after receiving the land, they have the freedom to use their land as per their own wish; not controlled by the landowners. Since there is no threat of eviction from the landowner, families are free to find their work and earn as per their own capacity. Families have a better negotiation power at the wage labour market. By increased income in the family, they have been able to create new assets for the use of productive purposes. Families have been able to give emphasis of sending their children to schools, capacity to save money for the future leading to prosperity.

International Food Policy Research Institute (IFPRI) in partnership with Landesa conducted a study in the state in 2012 to evaluate the impact of micro-plot allocation programme on women and their families and its contribution to food security. The key findings of the study indicate that including women's names on *patta* matters – it significantly contributes to women's perceptions of increased tenure security and to women's involvement in decision-making in the family regarding food consumption patterns and agricultural productions (what to produce and what extent). Women's report on tenure security outcomes improves up to 10 per cent when their names are included on the land documents. When women's name are on the *patta*, women are 14 per cent, 15 per cent, and 13 per cent more likely: to participate in decisions about taking loans, purchasing productive assets, and food purchasing and consumption, respectively.

Finally, women with *patta* in their names have say over a larger share of their households' land when it comes to decisions on how to use the land, what to grow on it, and whether or not to sell the produce from that. Moreover, the results of this study reflect that if their households are micro-plot beneficiaries, women are more likely to be involved in important food and agriculture decisions. Compared to their non-*patta* recipient peers, women in *patta* households are: *(a)* 12 per cent more likely to be involved in decisions to take loans from an SHG or micro finance institutions (MFI); *(b)* 12 per cent more likely to be involved in decisions on whether to purchase productive assets; *(c)* 9 per cent more likely to be involved in decisions regarding food purchase and consumptions; and *(d)* the share of the family land over which they are involved in decisions on how to use the land, what to grow on it, and whether to sell produce from it increased by 15 per cent, 14 per cent, and 11 per cent, respectively. Still, there is scope of conducting a comprehensive study to measure the impact of the programme in addressing poverty and landlessness in the state.

Road Ahead

The government has showed the commitment to conduct field level surveys to identify absolute landless families time to time. In spite of having huge pressure on land the government has made significant progress towards micro-plot allocation. The rest of the landless families identified by the LPLD Committees need to be covered. The government has also demonstrated political will to cover those by taking innovative policy decisions time to time like; purchasing *rayati* land where landless families have been residing etc. The government needs to take serious stand to implement convergence component of the programme in order to ensure holistic development of life and livelihoods of those families and help break the cycle of poverty.

The NGNB programme holds great promise for helping the poorest homesteadless and landless rural households to obtain a small plot of land on which they can construct a modest house, plant trees and vegetables, and raise poultry and small livestock. A homesteadless family that obtains land for a house gains important protection against eviction. And if the family can plan the optimal use of house-cum-garden by planting trees and keeping animals, the family is able thereby to supplement the family diet and perhaps supplement the family income from sale of garden production. In case of artisan families, a house and houschold enterprise can be of a great support in enhancing their socio-economic status. Homestead plots do not instantly create farmers – beneficiary families are likely to continue earning their main living through agricultural labour/or artisanship – but the plots do have the potential for greatly improving the family's livelihood in different ways. Thus, the programme can play instrumental role in addressing landlessness as well as the multi-dimensional aspects of rural poverty.

REFERENCES

1. Socio-economic Caste Census, 2011, Government of India.
2. India Rural Development Report 2012-13, IDFC Rural Development Network.
3. Planning Commission (2008). West Bengal State Development Report, Government of India.
4. Guidelines for Implementation of 'Nijo Griha Nijo Bhumi' Prakalpa (NGNB), Land and Land Reforms Department, Government of West Bengal.
5. Tim Hanstad, Roy Prosterman, Jennifer Brown (2002). Larger Homestead Plots as Land Reform?, *Economic and Political Weekly*, Vol. XXXVII, No. 29, July 20, 2002.
6. Tim Hanstad, T. Haque, Robin Nielsen (2008). Improving Land Access for India's Rural Poor, *Economic and Political Weekly*, Vol. XLIII, No. 10, March 8, 2008.
7. Hanstad, T., and Brown, J. (2001). Land Reform Law and Implementation in West Bengal: Lessons etc., and Recommendations. Seattle, WA, USA: Rural Development Institute.
8. R. Mitchell, T. Hanstad (2004). Small Homegarden Plots and Sustainable Livelihoods for the Poor, UNFAO Livelihood Support Programme, WP No. 11.
9. Florence Santos, Diana Fletschner, Vivien Savath, Amber Peterman (2014). Can Government-Allocated Land Contribute to Food Security? Intra-household Analysis of West Bengal's Microplot Allocation Programme, World Development Vol. 64, pp. 860-872, 2014.
10. The Millennium Development Goals Report, UN - 2014 http://www.un.org/millenniumgoals/2014%20MDG%20report/MDG%202014%20English%20web.pdf
11. World Bank, India (1997). Achievements and Challenges in Reducing Poverty.

Pages: 115-124

Rural Economy: *Changing Landscape*
Edited by: **Dr. Kartick Das**
ISBN: 978-93-5056-838-5
Edition: **2017**
Published by: **Discovery Publishing House Pvt. Ltd., New Delhi (India)**

Dry Land Farming
With Special Reference to Telangana

— **S. Vijay Kumar**

Dry land farming is an agricultural technique for non-irrigated cultivation of land. It may be defined as: 'a practice of growing profitable crops without irrigation in areas which receive an annual rainfall of 500 mm or even less'. India has about 108 million hectares of rain fed area which constitutes nearly 75 per cent of the total 143 million hectares of arable land. In India, dry land agriculture accounts for nearly two-thirds of total cropped area and generates nearly half of the total value of agricultural output. Rain fed agriculture encounters several constraints on account of climatic, edaphic, and social factors. Out of the 97 million farm holdings in India, about 76 per cent come under marginal and small categories. The productivity levels of these areas have remained lower across years because of frequent droughts occurring due to high variability in the quantum and distribution of rainfall, poor soil, low fertilizer use, imbalanced fertilization, small farm size and poor mechanization, poor socio-economic conditions and low risk-bearing capacity, low credit availability and infrastructure constraints. Consequently, farmers are distracted from agriculture and tend to migrate to cities to look for alternative jobs. Hence, there is a great need to increase the productivity of rain fed crops and overall net returns to keep the farmers in agriculture. A paradigm shift in rain fed agriculture can be expected through technological thrusts and policy changes. India has about 47 million hectares of dry lands out of 108 million hectares of total rain fed area. Dry lands contribute 42 per cent of the total food grain production of the country. These areas produce 75 per cent of pulses and more than 90 per cent of sorghum, millet, groundnut and pulses from arid and semi-arid regions. Thus, dry lands and rainfed farming will continue to play a dominant role in agricultural production.

Dry lands, besides being water deficient, are characterised by high evaporation rates, exceptionally high day temperature during summer, low humidity and high run off and soil erosion. The soils of such areas are often found to be saline and low in fertility. As water is the most important factor of crop production, inadequacy and uncertainty of rainfall often cause partial or complete failure of the crops which leads to period of scarcities and famines. Thus the life of both human being and cattle in such areas becomes difficult and insecure.

Despite all improvements in agriculture, we have not yet been able to evolve appropriate practices for our dry land areas. The income of farmers of dry land regions is low. We continue to stress on intensive agriculture on irrigated land but we cannot afford to be complacent with our dry lands. We cannot achieve stability in food production with unstabilized dry land agriculture. Therefore, we are required to adopt improved technology especially developed for dry land agriculture.

The Strategies that Need to be Emphasised

1. Land care and soil-quality improvement through conservation agricultural practices, balanced fertilization, harnessing the potential of bio-fertilizers and microorganisms, and carbon sequestration.
2. Efficient crops, cropping systems, and best plant types.
3. Management of land and water on watershed basis.
4. Adoption of a farming-systems approach by diversifying enterprises with high-income modules.
5. Mechanization for timely agricultural operations and precision agricultural approach.
6. Post-harvest, cold-storage, value-addition modules.
7. Assured employment and wage system.
8. Organic farming.
9. Rehabilitation of rain fed wastelands.
10. Policy changes and other support system.
11. Human-resource development, training and consultancy.

Characteristics of Dry-land Agriculture

Dry land areas may be characterised by the following features:

1. Uncertain, ill - distributed and limited annual rainfall.
2. Occurrence of extensive climatic hazards like: drought, flood etc.
3. Undulating soil surface.
4. Occurrence of extensive and large holdings.
5. Practice of extensive agriculture *i.e.,* prevalence of mono-cropping etc.
6. Relatively large size of fields.
7. Similarity in types of crops raised by almost all the farmers of a particular region.
8. Very low crop yield.
9. Poor market facility for the produce.
10. Poor economy of the farmers.
11. Poor health of cattle as well as farmers.

Problems of Dry Land Farming in India

The major problem which the farmers have to face very often is to keep the crop plants alive and to get some economic returns from the crop production. But this single problem is influenced by several factors, they are:

(i) *Moisture stress and uncertain rainfall*: The rains are very erratic, uncertain and unevenly distributed. Therefore, the agriculture in these areas has become a sort of gamble with the nature and very often the crops have to face climatic hazards. The farmers also take up farming halfheartedly as they are not sure of being able to harvest the crops. Thus, water scarcity becomes a serious bottleneck in dry land agriculture.

(ii) *Effective storage of rain water:* According to characteristics of dry farming, either there will be no rain at all or there will be torrential rain with very high intensity. Thus, in the former case the crops will have to suffer a severe drought and in the latter case they suffer either flood or water logging and they will be spoilt In case of very heavy downpour, the excess water gets lost as run-off which goes to the ponds and ditches etc. This water could be stored for providing life saving or protective irrigation to the crops grown in dry land areas. The loss of water takes place in several ways namely run-off, evaporation, uptake through weeds etc.

(iii) *Marketing problem*: In dry farming all the farmers grow similar crops which are drought resistant. These crops mature at the same time and the growers like to dispose off their products soon after the harvest. This results in a glut of products in the market and the situation is badly exploited by the grain traders and middlemen. Therefore, marketing becomes a serious problem in dry farming areas.

(iv) *Unbalance their economic position*: Only drought resistant crops namely: oilseeds, pulses and coarse grains like: jowar, bajra, millets etc., can be grown in dry land areas. Thus, the farmers have to purchase other food grains and household commodities that unbalance their economic position.

(v) *Careful and judicious manorial scheduling*: In case of irrigated farming the farmers are at a liberty to apply manures and fertilizers according to their availability and facility but in case of dry farming they have to be very careful in fertilizer application. Due to lack of available moisture, broadcasting or top dressing becomes wasteful and meaningless. These can be applied by only deep placement and foliar spray for an improved crop production.

(vi) *Utilization of preserved moisture:* Judicious and purposeful utilization of preserved moisture water depends upon soil type, plant type and other factors. The amount of available water to the plants depends upon the depth of plant roots, their proliferation and density. In case of limited moisture condition, the yield directly depends upon the rooting depth. The rooting depth can be desirably increased by mechanical manipulation of the soil. If the planting is very dense and all the plants have same kind of rooting then there will be a tough competition among roots for moisture and scarce moisture condition will result in the wilting of plants. Therefore, utilization of preserved moisture is an art in dry farming. The water collected in ponds or brooks may be used to give protective or life saving irrigation. The widely spaced crops can be intercropped with oilseeds or pulses for increasing the productivity of the land per unit area and per unit time. Therefore, the water collected during the rainy season need special technique and skill for its efficient utilization.

(vii) *Quality or-the produce:* The quality of the produce from dry farming areas is often found to be inferior as the grains are not fully developed or they are not filled properly; often mixed with other crop seeds owing to mixed .cropping system prevalent in these areas and the fodder become more fibrous. All these factors reduce the market value of produce and the farmers do not get the profit of their labour and investment.

Special Reference to Telangana

Telangana, the semi-arid land of India, is experiencing drought often pushing large numbers of people to the margins of living. Drought visits south Telangana 'once in two and half years'. The rainfall of about 70 cm and less in southern Telangana hardly justifies the fact that the region should languish under semi-arid conditions. In fact, the region forms part of the catchment of the perennial rivers Krishna and Godavari. The irrigation policy initiative over the years continuously favored the Delta region leaving a large number of people at the mercy of degraded nature and sub-human living. Thus "Telangana backwardness has essentially political roots: with better administration the considerable water resources could have been more fully tapped for irrigation. Telangana is still mainly a dry farming area; the reason for this in Telangana is long term failure to harness the potentialities of the area."

Analysis

As major irrigation facilities are not sufficiently available and short fall of normal rain, when compared to Costal Andhra region, Telangana is mostly dependent on dry land farming. In Telangana, in view of the non-availability of water in wells and tube wells due to depletion of water table and drought farmers are now forced to keep major part of their dry lands as current follow lands. As a result, the area under follow land is increasing year after year. There is a shift in cropping pattern and at the same time, the total area under jowar, bazra, caster and cereals decreased significantly, while the cultivable area under rice, maize, groundnut, oilseeds, cotton, pulses increased proportionately. The yield and production of these crops also increased. It is a definite change in favour of commercial crops.

Due to recurring drought conditions, most of the borrowers in rural areas of Telangana could not repay the loans borrowed earlier. In view of this, financial institutions kept those villages as de-faulted borrowers, included in the black list closing their chance of borrowing again. This has become a stumbling block to majority of the rural households in all the regions in the state, particularly in Telangana. Consequently, the dependency on money lenders and private financiers is again on the increase lending to increase in the cost of production, unremunerative cultivation and increasing indebtedness.

The State needs to give priority for agriculture particularly, in the field of irrigation sector and cheap and assured credit facility. The focus should be on dry land farming, extension services and provision of quality seeds and fertilizers and timely assistance. In recent years the plan allocations to the priority sectors such as: agriculture, irrigation has been declining from plan to plan. Irrigation sector is neglected.

Many of the proposed projects in Telangana region could not be undertaken. While total canal irrigation through canals remained stagnant, tank irrigation declined during the last two decades. Similarly, cultivation under dug wells and bore wells has increased significantly leading to power problems, and depleting water table below 600 feet in certain areas, and gradual withdrawal of subsidies to agricultural sector also increased cost of cultivation unremunerative cultivation. This has led to unrest among the farmers resulting suicide deaths especially in Telangana region.

Telangana projects have been allocated 266.83 TMC (Thousand Million Cubic Feet. One TMC ft is equivalent to about 28.317 million cubic meters or 22 956.8 acre feet) of water against a due share of 552 TMC. Mahboob Nagar known for its very high levels of distress migration and perennial drought should have got 187 TMC of water but have received nothing till now. Costal Andhra receives several times more than its due allocation of 99 TMC. Farming has become risky in Telangana, as indicated in the large number of suicides by farmers. Telangana accounts for as many as two- thirds (66%) of the total number of suicides reported in the state between 1998 and 2006. Though recent data shows that Telangana has been allocated a higher share in expenditure on irrigation (55%) than its share of population (41%) however, compared to costal Andhra, the unit cost of irrigation is much higher in Telangana (as it is situated in Deccan plateau) as lifting of water requires huge investments in pumping machinery and power.

As a matter of fact, majority of the households in villages are considered to be labourers. Real development of villages can only be achieved if the labour households' employment, wages and incomes are improved. It is observed that employment, wages and other living conditions of labour households are further deteriorated in recent times. Non-agricultural employment is found to be significant in those areas where canal irrigation is provided. With the development of agriculture, non-agricultural employment was also generated in the command areas. Due to backward agriculture and frequent droughts in most of the mandals of Telangana, labour households find it difficult to get employment during lean seasons and prefer to migrate to far and near places. The process of migration has accelerated in recent years. Due to lopsided developmental strategies pursued from time to time, balanced development of the state has become a casualty and regional imbalances went on widening. These imbalances have become stumbling blocks for the emotional integration of the people of all the three regions of the state. Further, the process of implementation of economic reforms including privatisation is taking place at an accelerated pace in the state.

Impact of Liberalization, Privatization and Globalization

The policies of liberalization, privatization and globalization have been displacing thc masses from their opportunities. The benefits and subsidies meant for weaker sections are reduced year after ycar even these meant for the Scheduled Castes and Scheduled Tribes. This is not followed by a corresponding support in alternative occupations or opportunities. With introduction of labour saving technology in the field of construction of roads and buildings, wage labourers have been badly affected in the state. In view of the lopsided pattern of development, the state has been witnessing agitations, movements, rural unrest, farmer suicides and hunger deaths in recent years. The village economy is facing economic and social crisis. Agriculture is unable to absorb the over increasing working population. Further, the cost of production per unit of agricultural output in Andhra Pradesh now is higher compared to major agricultural States in India. The area under canal irrigation system declined due to deceleration in public investment in Telangana. In nutshell, the agricultural sector is neglected by thc government. There is a need to review this policy.

Small and marginal farmers have been worst effected. Majority of the small and marginal farmers still depend in informal or non-institutional sources of credit, particularly, money lenders, private financiers at higher rates of interest, consequently, high cost of production and indebtedness.

Liberalization and Privatization process was initiated in the state with firm determination during 1996-97. But its impact is not well received by all section of the people. Agricultural growth rates have gone down drastically. Employment situation in rural areas were not improved rather deteriorated. Whatever the employment opportunities have been created so far, they are largely low paid and casual in nature and insecure. Nonagricultural employment could not be generated to the levels of expectations. Villages have become markets for products of multinational and big industries. Whatever the industries or small scale industrial units were available earlier, they are unable to compete with global products either in quality or prices. Backward area like: Telangana (except Hyderabad) could not attract either domestic or foreign direct investment.

There is an exodus of young persons from villages of backward and drought effected districts to towns and cities in search of livelihood. People from Mahaboobnagar, Nalgonda, Karimnagar, Warangal and Medak are migrating to gulf countries and Hyderabad to get some livelihood or other. Only old age people keep staying in rural areas. The Information and Technology could provide jobs to a few thousands of educated young people.

The Self help Groups for women could not provide work as expected. This programme could enlighten rural women groups in political and social aspects. These groups could mobilize savings out of their hard earned income besides State/Central assistance. As far as employment and income generation activity of this programme is concerned, very little is achieved. Whatever the products are produced by these groups, they are decorative and artistic, unable to compete with global multinational products. Mostly they are neither mass consumption oriented nor essentials. Hence, they suffer from lack of demand. The scheme has become political wing of ruling party for vote bank.

Suggestions

1. Agriculture may be given top priority along with infrastructure development in backward regions. Constructions of Ichampally irrigation project across river Godavari will benefit north Telangana. Similarly, through proper allocation and utilisation of Krishna river water will also benefit Nalgonda, Mahabubnagar districts in South Telangana.
2. Distribution of cultivable public lands surplus lands and cultivable waste lands among the rural poor provides some solution to the agricultural labourers.
3. There is an urgent need to change the cropping pattern in drought prone areas of the regions to prevent further downslide of underground water table.
4. It is also necessary to identify backward districts and specific area programmes may be initiated through state and central grants.
5. Rural and agricultural credit facilities have to be adequately provided to all the needy households keeping in view the growing dependency of farmers and rural artisans on money lenders and private financiers.
6. Both central financial transfers and use of policy instruments will be useful to attract private investment to the backward regions.
7. Enhanced allocations for social development such as: education, health, nutrition, empowerment of poor. Further democratization of rural institutions etc., will improve education, skills and entrepreneurial abilities of people in backward areas.

Conclusion

Even after utilizing all the available water resources, about 50 per cent of our cultivable area will still depend on rains. Therefore, our agricultural scientists, policy formulators and farmers should appropriately realize the magnitude of role that rainfed agriculture or dryland farming can play. They should thoroughly examine the problems of dry land agriculture from different viewpoints and evolve appropriate technologies, crop varieties, etc., for these areas to better the economic position of the farmers. Dry farming areas, therefore, need a much closer attention for achieving food security in India.

REFERENCES

1. Jodha NS. (1996). Ride the Crest or Resist the Change? Response to Emerging Trends in Rainfed Farming Research in India, *Economic and Political Weekly*, 13 July 1996.
2. Gadgil M and Guha R. (1993). This Fissured Land: An Ecological History of India. Delhi: Oxford University Press.
3. Development of Irrigation', New Delhi 'Development of Drought-prone Areas' (DDPA), p. 47.
4. Forrester, D.B. (1970). 'Sub-regionalism in India: The Case of Telangana', Pacific Affairs, Vol. XI, No. 111, p. 8.
5. 'Perspectives on Telangana – I' (1997). Telangana Information Trust, Hyderabad.
6. 'The Movement for Telangana', EPW, pp. 9 and 10, Jan. 9-15, 2010.
7. Pattern of Development in India - A Study of Andhra Pradesh SER Division Planning Commission Government of India.
8. Gadgil M and Guha R. (1993). This Fissured Land: An Ecological History of India. Delhi: Oxford University Press.

Pages: 125-134

Rural Economy: *Changing Landscape*

Edited by: **Dr. Kartick Das**

ISBN: 978-93-5056-838-5

Edition: **2017**

Published by: **Discovery Publishing House Pvt. Ltd., New Delhi (India)**

Saga of 'Noodle Doodles'

An Analysis of Do's and Don'ts During Crisis Communication with Reference to Nestle India's Maggi Noodles

— **Vijayalakshmi Kanteti**

INTRODUCTION

Nestlé India Ltd. (NIL), the Indian subsidiary of the global FMCG major, Nestlé SA, introduced the Maggi brand in India in 1982, with its launch of Maggi 2 Minute Noodles, an instant noodles product, which were not previously part of the culinary culture, and instant food was not common in the Indian packaged food market. Maggi became the breakfast of choice for parents struggling to get their children ready for school in the morning. The advertised idea of a delicious and nutritional meal that could be cooked in just two minutes appealed to millions. Maggi became a preferred snack for children, singletons and working couples. In more recent years, hundreds of thousands of Maggi stalls have opened across the country making it a popular street food. Urbanization, rising income levels, working couples, interstate migration and changing lifestyle of young India are key drivers for the noodles market. The product was positioned as a meal which is filling and can be prepared in just a few minutes, thus offering both convenience and time saving.

Now, India is the second largest single market for Nestle's Maggi brand, with retail sales worth $623 million in 2014 across noodles, table sauces and other products, according to Euromonitor International. Nestle has virtually dominated the Indian noodle market till now but lately many large FMCG players and retail chains like:

Hindustan Unilever (knorr soupy noodles), Glaxo smithkline consumer healthcare (Foodles), capital Foods Ltd. (Ching's secret), ITC (sunfest yippee noodles), Future group (tasty treat) have launched their products in this lucrative space. Still Maggi holds a commanding position in the Noodles Segment with over 70 per cent market share. Maggi has a large fan following in the country and personalities such as: Amitabh Bachchan have endorsed it in the past. Because of its first-mover advantage, NIL successfully managed to retain its leadership in the instant noodles category.

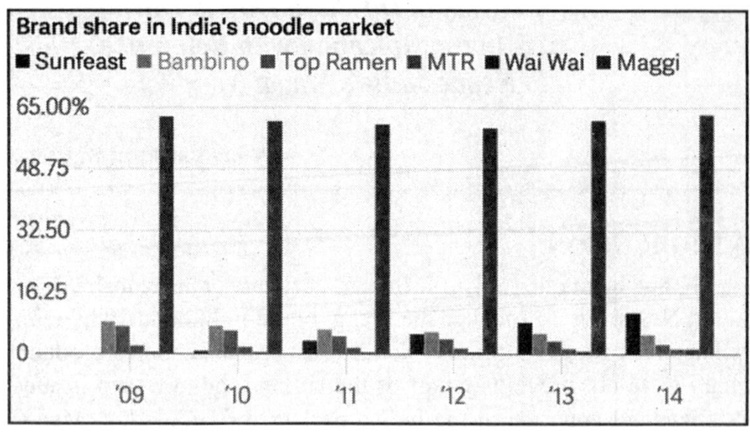

Source: Quartz qz.com

Such a stalwart brand is caught hold in the noodle doodle soup crisis at present. Most of the damage has happened because the brand failed to communicate. The present case tries to identify the issues related to the crisis management as well as how and what Maggi could have done to resolve the crisis through proper communication strategies at the earliest.

Background of the Case

The brand that commanded an over 70 per cent of the market share in the instant noodles category, beat a hasty retreat in the wake of reports by FSSAI (The Food Safety and Standards Authority of India) which was established under Food Safety and Standards Act, 2006 for laying down science based standards for articles of food and to regulate their manufacture, storage, distribution, sale and import to ensure availability of safe and wholesome food for human consumption. Testing in Government Laboratories in UP and Kolkata revealed that one of India's favorite snacks had 7 times the permissible amount of MSG or monosodium glutamate otherwise popularly known as Ajinomoto, a taste enhancer. Elemental lead has also been detected of up to 17.2 parts per million. FDA officials seized more than 2 lakh packets of various quantities of Maggi Noodles. FDA officials from other states have begun conducting similar raids and samples of the product have been sent for testing.

Recent samples from UP, Bihar and few other states have shown excessive lead that leads to many damaging attributes among children primarily resulting in by nationwide ban for Nestle's Meri Maggi. Mistakes happen. Really. So why doesn't Nestle own up? Why don't they release 'more' than a press release and actually TALK to consumers? What happened? This happened with Coke happened with Cadbury. So why is this on such a bigger scale as compared to others?

Company's Stand on the Issue

According to the Company CEO Paul Bulcke, Nestle's product was 'safe for consumption'. The Nestle site states "Nestlé India has tested around 1,000 batches of MAGGI Noodles in their own laboratories and also asked an independent lab to test an additional 600 product batches. These tests covered batches totaling 125 million or 12.5 Crore packets of noodles in total. These tests found that levels of lead in the products were within the food safety limits specified by the Indian authorities."

With the Government forcing a nationwide ban for Nestle on 3rd June, 2015; India is planning to sue Nestle for damages, it is the first time India taking on legal actions against a multi-national company. With the ban, over 500 workers at the Maggi Factory lost their jobs, big companies like: Nestle holds a strong hand on a country's economy. However, Merri Maggi is only 1 per cent of Nestle's global sales, but the damage to its brand worldwide is immeasurable.

Flow of Communication Stating how the Crisis Cooked up

The first notice which Nestle India got for unhealthy food practices and deceitful labelling was in March 2014. That is 15 months back. In July last year, Nestle appealed regarding the issue and Maggi was sent for testing in the Kolkata Central Food Laboratory, a NABL accredited government lab. In April this year when the results found high levels of lead and MSG, Nestle did not even respond the FDA warnings. Nestle may have assumed that the government would be indifferent, that the media would move on, and the controversy would die a natural death. They were wrong.

The startling findings of lead and MSG in Maggi were confirmed in April 2015, the mainstream media picked up the issue, a month later, on 20th May 2015.

There was a one month window for the food giant to get its act together.

21st May 2015 – Indian State Orders Recall of Maggi Noodles

Indian food inspectors order Nestlé India to recall a batch of Maggi Noodles from the northern Indian state of Uttar Pradesh claiming that tests have found Maggi instant noodles 'unsafe and hazardous' and accused Nestlé of failing to comply with food safety law.

Nestlé Response

The initial response from the global FMCG Company rejected the accusation that the noodles were unsafe and said on their website and social media accounts that there had been no order to recall any products.

A statement on their website said that "The quality and safety of our products are the top priorities for our Company. We have in place strict food safety and quality controls at out Maggi factories. We do not add MSG to Maggi Noodles, and glutamate, if present, may come from naturally occurring sources. We are surprised with the content supposedly found in the sample as we monitor the lead content regularly as a part of the regulatory requirements."

1st June – Nestlé Re-assures Customers its Noodles are Safe

Nestlé continues to keep its customers up to date on the investigation into the safety of Maggi noodles in India. On the official Maggi noodles India Facebook page, Twitter and website, Nestlé states that extensive testing reveals no excess lead in Maggi noodles.

2nd June – Nestlé Interacts with Customers on Social Media Thanking them for their Support

Nestlé uses Twitter and Facebook to answer customers questions about the levels of MSG and lead found in their noodles. The company continues to re-assure customers that the noodles are safe and that they are a transparent company working closely with authorities in India to resolve the issue. As well as this Nestlé explains the science behind the tests, what lead and MSG are and gives an informative breakdown of the ingredients in their product.

Findings and Implications for Crisis Communication

- ***The First Response cannot be Denial in Crisis Communication***

This is the age of consumer activism, Conditional acceptance of allegations can work wonders in limiting potential damage. Nestle continues to remain in denial. Its argument: Maggi is safe. But an offer to recall or withdraw existing stocks from shop shelves immediately after the controversy broke out could have prevented things getting out of hand. Nestlé defended its product and rejected all claims that its noodles were unsafe, and they did this on all digital channels for which it later apologized.

Nestle India has chosen to brazen it out. It has stated that MSG is found in the raw materials used to make the noodles. That lead is present in the soil and atmosphere! This brings back memories of how Cadbury blamed retailers for poor storage of chocolates that were found to be contaminated. It would be well to remember that in that case Cadbury was forced to accept responsibility, change its packaging and bring in Indian movie superstar Amitabh Bachchan to redeem its brand. The cost; loss of sales during the Diwali festival season. For a situation of this magnitude, the Nestle global site does not even acknowledge the controversy in India..

- ***Maggi was Slow in Reaction to the Crisis***

It is important for an organization to move at the speed of the crisis and not their own 'business as usual' speed. In the digital era, a day late is like being a month late. Maggi enjoyed the special status because of their consumers. Maggi needed to behave responsibly and hence instead of negating the issue, it should have immediately offered to take back the stocks from effected markets, issuing a statement proactively something like "In view of the current issues as reported in the media, we are calling our stocks back to check and rectify the issue, we will validate our product's safety and then only would bring back the product in market. Absence of communication by Nestle horrified image management specialists.

In fact while the controversy was at its peak, Maggi's regular Television commercial (The schoolgirl, 'Rajkumari' - Mom Ad) was constantly being aired across channels depicting an attitude as if the company was under the impression that the trouble was minor and would blow away at worse. The company appeared to be in denial-mode without, however, stating its position in so many words.

After meeting with the national food safety regulators, Nestlé said it was withdrawing Maggi noodles from stores 'despite the product being safe'. Almost simultaneously, the national food safety regulator ordered Nestlé to recall all Maggi noodles from store shelves.

- ***Could have been Proactive Rather than being Forced to be Reactive***

Being conservative is good, but not quite in a crisis involving its most iconic product. They could've recalled the product voluntarily (Nestle did that in USA in 2014 over one complaint of incorrect packaging of Häagen-Dazs ice-cream), and come clean saying that the safety of Indians takes precedence over everything else.

They kept quiet about the issue for three whole weeks, even though facing a demand from regulators to recall the product. Three weeks later Nestlé's leadership bowed to the inevitable after facing a social media storm. The company issued a tardy press release on 21 May admitting receiving a recall order, but then offered a denial carrying little conviction.

This defensive response was treated with the disdain it deserved. Responding to public anger, several states ordered tests and started issuing bans on the sale of Maggi noodles.

It would have been best for Nestle India to adopt a cautious posture and state that they would conduct an inquiry into the matter. They could have been proactive and taken off Maggi voluntarily from shelves for some time. This was what Johnson and Johnson did when they had a crisis due to Tylenol poisoning in the US in 1982. It was later found out to be a case of sabotage. But the prompt and proactive action was rewarded by the public and the brand of Johnson and Johnson received a major boost. Now Nestle India has been given government orders in various states to take off Maggi off shelves. This is a major loss of face, not to mention the financial loss.

- ***Lack of a Trained Spokes Person who can be a 'Human Face'***

There does not seem to be a human face behind communications of Nestle India. They are dealing with the media through statements to the press. At a time like this, a senior person from Nestle India should have led from the front so that consumers could gain some trust in the management of Nestle India. For any damage control there should be a trained spokesperson, preferably a senior creditable one, to face the media. Maggi's spokespersons were not available to comment on the issue but Maggi ads were being played in prime time on GECs hammered further that the brand cares for nothing. It came across as arrogant and irresponsible rather than being 'a dear trusted friend' that brand had personified itself as, in the last three decades.

- ***Lack of Empathy***

Maggi has an emotional bond with consumers; brand already has a tremendous amount of emotional connect. All communication from Nestle India so far seems to lack empathy for its customers. It seems merely interested in technical repudiation of allegations rather than empathizing with the consumers of its products and reassuring them that the right thing will be done.

The CEO could have put out a two part video. One part where he is having a Maggi meal at home with family and at office with colleagues. The other part where he is talking about the confidence the company has in the product and its safety which would connect emotionally with the consumers.

- ***Engage with all Forms of Media to Communicate***

Nestle is treating this as a local problem. But Indians are everywhere. Really big on social media. It would be a rude shock to consumers elsewhere if they discovered that Maggi was being withdrawn in India but continued in their countries.

The company needs to bring out front-page advertisements because the opportunity to enjoy earned media has gone away. These ads should run for a week educating consumers about the action being taken and the goodness of the product. With the kind of market share Maggi enjoyed and the revenues it brought in it would not be a bad idea for the global CEO to fly down and meet the authorities.

It needs to use social media to interact smartly and there are several recent examples of cases where the brand custodians have defended products vigorously on the online medium. None of this is rocket science and it is surprising that Nestle has not taken the basic steps during a crisis. Maggi is a good example of how a brand takes twenty years to build and just two minutes to get destroyed.

There was clearly need of urgent crisis communication. A brand that had been communicating actively did nothing for days to communicate their point of view about the crisis. Maggi officials couldn't really gauge the gravity of the crisis, probably they were confident about their product and thought that news would die down on its own or they were completely clueless what to do as it was first of its kind situation for them. The fact remains Maggi failed to communicate with consumers who had trusted the company and product for such a long time.

In this age of 24x7 television and social media, organizations get slammed by negative publicity. There is a need for the organization to be present on various media and be part of the conversation. While Nestle India has built Maggi as a brand through countless TV commercials, they are yet to put out an infomercial that addresses the current crisis. Their response on social media seems non-existent.

To make it more acceptable to its stakeholders and consumers, the results should be made public through banners and advertisements wherever possible, besides of course the social media. In short it should start talking to consumers and demonstrate that it cares.

Till such tests can be undertaken, it should put up banners and posters in every point of purchase and even billboards about the ingredients it uses and overall product safety. Films and TV ads should highlight the production processes and the steps it takes to ensure product safety and consumer health.

Their social media response was a disaster. Robotic replies, sharing heavy PDF files in the name of responses; Nestle India's social media damage control has been a joke. Just look at the cookie-cutter responses in the photo below, clearly Nestle India was unwilling to establish consumer connect.

The following conversation on twitter shows the monotonous style of communication by Maggi India.

They blocked all lines of communication with consumers. For more than a fortnight, barring a computer-generated statement, there was no word from Nestle. Nearly all beat journalists, wrote and re-wrote to Nestle for a more human, in-depth response, but Nestle was too arrogant for a 2-minute reply.

- ***Draft a Crisis Management Plan well in Advance***

This is not the first or last time that organizations will stumble in face of a crisis. The key to handing crisis effectively is planning. The language of credibility has a different grammar. Media-mass and social-plays the role of conjunction in this dialect. Grabbing eyeballs

Chart 1 Showing the social media communication on twitter

24x7 is important. Crisis communications, like all other crisis responses, should be drafted before hand. It is unclear whether this is really a case of lack of planning or poor execution of a crisis management plan. It would be shocking if a large organization like Nestle India had not planned for this scenario. A more likely possibility is that they may have had the plans but never exercised the plans leading to poor execution.

- ***Constant Communication as an Educative Tool***

Each brand has a soul and a distinct character. That's what distinguishes a cult brand (say a Harley Davidson mobike) from an average brand. Constant education about the brand is a standard operating procedure to keep crisis at bay.

Nestle's representatives have been hardly seen either at retail stores or popular vends offering to clear the air. Neither has it come out with any unusual videos or campaigns to educate loyal patrons.

Nestle India could look at roping in a brand ambassador to advocate their products. The ambassador or the celebrity should have high trust value amongst the audiences. Coca-Cola and Cadbury roped in Amir Khan and Amitabh Bachchan respectively during their time of crisis.

Maggi has been in the market for years. They can reveal statistics of deaths due to Maggi over the past decade which would be none. Hence using numbers as a positive reinforcement. Make necessary changes to the product and that adhere to the norms. Co-operate with the FDA and redress the issue. Build a campaign around Maggi being a health conscious brand through its latest wheat, oat and raggi noodles.

The Road Ahead

Though recently, the Bombay High Court has ruled, new tests are required to prove that the popular snack does not contain excess lead and lifted the ban for time being, Nestle has been told that over the next six weeks, it must have five samples of its noodles tested by three accredited labs to prove the amount of lead is within permissible limits. If the tests are in Nestlé's favor, it can start selling the noodles again. Nestle obviously cannot ignore the gravity of the situation they are in. Maggi has lost the trust of many customers and rebuilding that trust will be a challenge for Nestle. There is an immense window of opportunity for Maggi's rival brands. One can derive that the crisis will most certainly have an impact on Nestlé's revenue. Maggi's approach to crisis came across as irresponsible quite contrary to its personification of being a dear friend. Lack of communication and 'wait n watch' strategy of Maggi officials proved fatalistic for the brand and its imagery. Consumers felt cheated and it probably would leave the scars for a long time to come.

REFERENCES

1. www.linkedin.com/pulse/maggi-crisis-management-lessons-learned keith-prabhu
2. www.economictimes.indiatimes.com/articleshow/47599502.
3. www.ethicalcorp.com/stakeholder-engagement/asia-column-lessons-nestles-crisis-india
4. www.digitalstrategyconsulting.com
5. www.netimperative.com/2015/07/crisis-management-case-study-nestles-maggi-noodles-banned-in-india
6. www.nestle.in/about us/ask-nestle/answers/maggi-noodles-india-safe
7. www.hindustantimes.com/business-news/5-things-nestle-should-have-done-to-combat maggi-crisis-a-poor-show-in-crisis-management
8. www.theresearchpedia.com/research-articles/indian-noodle-market
9. www.nestle.in

Pages: 135-144

Rural Economy: *Changing Landscape*
Edited by: **Dr. Kartick Das**
ISBN: 978-93-5056-838-5
Edition: **2017**
Published by: **Discovery Publishing House Pvt. Ltd., New Delhi (India)**

Pradhan Mantri Krishi Sinchayee Yojana
A Game Changer Project for Agriculture

— **Anil Kumar Biswas**

The total population of India, as in March 2015, is 128, 27, and 41,906. The country accounts for 17.31 per cent of the world's population. At present one out of six persons in this planate lives in India. According to UN report the growth of the population in India has assumed alarming proportion and, if the present trends persist, it will almost double in the next 20 years. It will be figured around 2.56 billion. According to 2011, census 68.9 per cent, which is more than 83 crore, lived in rural India. Majority of the population of India depends on agriculture and agriculture related works for their livelihood. Rural economy fully depends on agriculture and agriculture related works. Day to day population is increased and land holding patterns are decreased. So it is very necessary to increase sustainable productivity of the crops in existing land. At present 141 hector net area shown in our country. Out of them about 65 million hectare, which is any 45 per cent lands of total area is presently covered by under irrigation. So, maximum agricultural lands are even today out of irrigation coverage. Most of the farmers of the country even today depend on monsoon rain water for their crops production. So they always had fallen in an uncertain situation. Due to lack of proper management monsoon rain water are fully misused so it is very necessary to taken a proper policy for coverage of all lands under irrigation and extension of coverage present agricultural lands. For this aim government of India has taken various policy programmers' for the increasing of sustainable agricultural productivity. During the 12th five-year plan in order to maintain target growth rate of four per cent in agriculture the department has been restructure into five missions. Such missions are: *(i)* National Food Security Mission (NFSM), *(ii)* Mission for Integrated Development of Horticulture (MIDH), *(iii)* National Mission on Oil Seeds and Oil Palm (NMOOP), *(iv)* National Mission for Sustainable Agricultural (NMSA), *(v)* National Mission on Agricultural Extension and Technology (NMAET) and other four central sector schemes such as: *(i)* National Crop Insurance Programme (NCIP), *(ii)* Integrated Scheme on Agri-Census and Statistic (ISAC&S), *(iii)* Integrated Scheme of Agriculture Marketing (ISAM), *(iv)* Integrated Scheme of Agriculture Cooperation (IAC) and also one State Plan Rastriya Krishi Vikas Yojana (RKVY). The Union Budget of 2014-15 lays emphasis on agriculture for the inclusive economic growth. For this the budgets has emphasised need for measures to make farming a competitive and profitable activity. The provisions of Kisan Television, Warehouse infrastructure Fund, Price Stabilization Fund, Kisan Vikas Patra and long term Rural Credit Fund in NABARD and intention to user in second green revolution with focus on higher productivity are clear indicators of sincere efforts to encourage agriculture sector in the economy. Very recently government has taken some new policy initiative for the improvement of the agriculture sector. Such policies are: *(i)* Soil Health Card Scheme, *(ii)* Pradhan Mantri Krishi Sinchayee Yojona; *(iii)* Price Stabilization Fund for Cereals and Vegetables; *(iv)* National Agri-Tech Infrastructure. From these, Pradhan Mantri Krishi Sinchayee Yojona is one of the most important policy projects for the development of the irrigation sector.

Pradhan Mantri Krishi Sinchayee Yojona (PMKSY)

Honorable president of India in his address to the joint season of Parliament on 16th Lok Sabha highlighted that each drop of water is precious. Government is giving high priority to water security. For this motto government launch the 'Pradhan Mantri Krishi Sinchayee Yojona' for the development of irrigation sector. The Cabinet Committee on Economic Affairs, chaired by the Prime Minister of India has given its approval to this new scheme (PMKSY). Government has estimated and outlays Rs. 50,000 crore cover a period of five years, which is 2015-16 to 2019-20. The allocation for the current financial year is Rs. 5300 crore. There is including options for the development of the irrigation sector under this scheme. There are option for linking rivers for ensuring optimal use of our water resources and to prevent the recurrence of floods and drought. Harnessing rain water through 'Jal Santa' and 'Jal Sinchan' also included under this scheme for water conservation and ground water recharge. Micro irrigation projects also included under this mega policy projects for the improvement of irrigation sector on the motto of 'Per drop – More Crops'. But qucstion is why now needs us types of policy programme for the improvement of the irrigation sector? The answer is most of the farmers in our country till today depends on rain water for crops production. Till today near about half of the total lands lays out of irrigation facility. There are so many causes' behinds these facts. Till independence irrigation sector was a net sources of revenue for the British Government. So irrigation sector was not set-up by the British government on the interest of the public demands on that time. During the second half of the 19th century British Government was taken some initiative for irrigation sector. There was also another cause behind this initiative. Due to cause of draught it was need to provide crops protection saving their expenditure on famine relief. So it is clear the irrigation sector was not so sound at the time of British era. As a result the irrigated land was only 22.6 Million hectares in 1950-51. This scenario is not so well even till today ,because at present it covers 65 million lands ,which is only 45 per cent of total land.

After independence planned development era has started and focus shifted from purely revenue generation to rapid harnessing of Water resources for multiple benefits. Consequently, the State governments were encouraged to expeditiously formulate and implements water resources projects for specific purpose like: irrigation, flood control, hydro-power generation, and drinking water supply, industrial and other miscellaneous uses. Since then there are so many initiative has taken by the government for the development, improvement and renovations of irrigation sector. Pradhan Mantri Krishi Sinchayee Yojona (PMKSY) is another strong policy projects taken by the Central Government for the rapid development, improvement and expansion of irrigation facilities.

Objectives of the Pradhan Mantri Krishi Sinchayee Yojana (PMKSY)

The major objects of the Pradhan Mantri Krishi Sinchayee Yojana are:

- Achieve coverage of investments in irrigation at the field level; such as: preparation of District Level Plan and if required Block Level Plan.
- Enhance the physical excess of water on the farm and expand cultivable area under assured irrigation in the motto of 'Har khet ko Pani'.
- Integration of water sources distribution and its efficient use, to make best use of water through appropriate technologies and practices.
- Improve on-farm water on the farm and expand use efficiency to reduce wastage and increase availability both in duration and extent.
- Enhance the adoption of precision - irrigation and other water saving technologies in the motto of 'more crop per drop'.
- Enhance recharge of aquifers and introduced sustainable water conservation practice.
- Ensure the integrated development of rain fed areas using the watershed approach towards soil and water conservation, regeneration of ground water, arresting runoff, providing livelihood options.
- Promote extension activities relating to water harvesting, water management and crop alignment for farmers and the grassroots level field functionaries.
- Explore the feasibility of reusing treated municipal waste water for peri-urban agriculture.
- Attract grater private investment in agriculture.

Strategy and Coverage area of the PMKSY

To achieve the objectives PMKSY will strategise by focusing on end-to end solution in irrigation supply chain *i.e.* Water sources, distribution networks, efficient farm level applications, extension on new technologies and information etc. These scheme broadly coverage on:

- Creation of new water sources; repair, restoration and innovation of defunct water sources. Construction of water harvesting structures ,secondary and micro storage, ground water development, enhancing potentials of traditional water bodies at village levels like: as 'Jal Mandir' in Gujarat; 'Khatri kuhl' in Himachal Pradesh; 'Zabo' in Nagaland; 'Eri', 'Ooranish' in Tamil Nadu; 'Dongs in Assam: 'Katash' in Odisha; and 'Bandhes in Madhya Pradesh.
- Developing/augmenting distribution network where irrigation sources are available or created.
- Promotion of scientific moisture conservation and run off. Control measure to improve ground water recharge so as to create opportunities for farmer to access recharged water through shallow tube/dug wells.
- Promoting efficient water conveyance and field application devices within the farm such as: underground piping system, drip and sprinklers, pivots, rain-guns and other application devices etc.
- Encouraging community irrigation through registered user groups/farmer producer's organizations/NGO's.
- Farmer oriented activities like: capacity building training and exposure visits, demonstrations, farm school, skill development in efficient water and crop management practices including large scale awareness or 'more crop per drop' of water through mass media campaign, exhibitions, field days and extension activities through short animation films etc.

Programme Components of the PMKSY

PMKSY has brought some irrigation related programme under one roof for the better result. The main programme components of the Pradhan Mantri Krishi Sinchayee Yojona are:

- Accelerated Irrigation benefits programme (AIBP).
- PMSKY on the motto of 'Har Khet KO Pani'.
- PMKSY in the motto of 'Per drop more crop' vision.
- PMKSY in the vision of watershed development.
- Under Accelerated Irrigation Benefits Programme the main aim of the PMSKY is to focus on faster competition ongoing major and medium irrigation including national projects.

The main aim of the Pradhan Mantri Krishi Sinchayee Yojona (Har Khet KO Pani) is focuses on:

- Creation of new water sources through minor Irrigation.
- Repair, restoration and renovation of water bodies; strengthening carrying capacity of traditional water sources, construction of rain Water harvesting structures.
- Command area development ,strengthening and creation of distribution network from the sources to the farm.
- Ground water development in the areas where it is abundant, so that sink is created to store run off/flood water during peak rainy season.
- Improvement in water management and distribution system for water bodies to take advantages of the available sources. Which is not tapped to its fullest capacity.
- Diversion of water from sources of different location where it is plenty to nearby water scare areas.
- Creating and rejuvenating traditional water storage systems of the country.
- The main aim of the Pradhan Mantri Krishi Sinchayee (Per Drop More crop) is focus on:
- Promoting efficient water conveyance and precision water application devices like: drips, sprinklers, pivots and rain guard in the form.
- Construction of micro irrigation structures to supplement sources creation activities including tube wells and dug wells which are not supported under AIBP, PMSKY, (Har Khet KO Pani), PMKSY (watershed) and MGNREGS as per block/distinct irrigation plan.
- Secondary storage structures at tail end of conceal system to store water when available in abundance on from perennial sources like streams for use during dry periods through effective on-farm water management.
- Extension activities for promotion of scientific moisture conservation and agronomic measures including cropping alignment to maximize use of available water including rainfall and minimize irrigation requirements.

- Capacity building, training, and awareness campaign including low cost publications, use of Pico projectors and low cost films for encouraging potential use water sources through technological, agronomic and management practices including community irrigation.
- The extension workers will be empowered to disseminate relevant technologies under PMKSY only after requisite training is provided to them especially in the area of promotion of scientific moisture conservation and agronomic measures, improved/innovative distribution system like: pipe and box outlet system etc.
- Introduction communication technology interventions through NEGPA to made use in the field of water use efficiency, precession irrigation technology, on forms water management, Crop alignment etc., and also to do intensive monitoring of the scheme.

The main aim of the Pradhan Mantri Krishi Sinchayee (water Shed development) is focuses on:

- Effective management of rain off water and improved soil and moisture conservation activities such as: ridge area treatment, drainage line treatment, rain water harvesting and other allied activities on water shed basis.
- Converging with MGNREGS for creation of water source to full potential in identified backward rain field blocks including renovation of traditional water bodies.

Structural Planning of PMSKY Scheme

The architecture of the Pradhan Mantri Krishi Sinchayee Yojana set up two structure planning *i.e. (i)* District irrigation plan and *(ii)* State Irrigation plan for the aim of decentralized planning. District irrigation plans shall be the cornerstone for planning and implementation of PMKSY. It will identify the gaps in irrigation infrastructure after taking into consideration the Pradhan Mantri Krishi Sinchayee Yojana. District irrigation plan will have holistic development perspective of the distinct outlining medium to long-term developmental plans integrating three components namely-water source, distribution of network and water use application incorporating all uses of water like: drinking and domestic use, irrigation and industry. The district irrigation plan prepared at two levels – the block and the district levels. Keeping in view the convenience of map preparation and data collection, the work would be primarily done at block levels. Block wise irrigation plan is to be prepared depending on the available and potential water resources and water requirement for agriculture sector prioritizing the activities based on socio-economic and location specific requirement. In case of planning is based on basin/sub basin level the comprehensive irrigation plan may cover more than district. The block level master plan is to be approved by intermediate level Block Panchayat and to be forwarded to the district planning committee for inclusion in the distinct master plan *i.e.* District Irrigation Plan, Technical, financial and human resources for this sector are supported from the departments of Rural Development, Urban Development ,Drinking water, Environment and Forest, Science and Technology, Industrial policy etc. The district irrigation plans are to be vetted by the governing body of Zilla Panchayat and subsequently be incorporated in the state irrigation plan. Each District will be provided one time financial support to purchase District Irrigation Plan. District Irrigation Plan will be finalized within a period of three months from launching of PMKSY.

State Irrigation Plan Consolidated the district irrigation plan and correlate with state agriculture plan available for RKVY. Apart from these the state irrigation plan prioritizes resources and outline definite annual action plan with medium to long term horizon. The plan would also enumerated on extension and ICT related activities to be undertaken under supervision of Agricultural Technology Management Agency. State irrigation plan and also district irrigation plan will provide requisite emphasis on convergence by eliminating overlap of resources and efforts and ensuring optimal utilization of funds available through various centrally sponsored and state plan schemes. National Rain fed Area Authority will be associated in preparation of state irrigation plan and providing advisories to state government for comprehensive irrigation development.

Funding Pattern of PMKSY

PMKSY's funds will be provided to the state governments as per the pattern of the assistance of centrally sponsored schemes decided by Ministry of Finance and NITI Aayog. During 2015-16 the government has sanctioned Rs. 5300 crore for this purpose and Rs. 50,000 crore estimated for a period of five year from 2015-16 to 2019-20. 50 per cent priority will be given for the project to those districts having larger share of un-irrigated areas, lesser agriculture productivity, proportion of the population of SCs/STS and small and marginal farmers. The remaining 50 per cent priority will be given to the operationalising/structuring projects which are under terminal stage of completion. Priority also to be given for reducing the gap between irrigation potential created and actually utilised through command area development and precision irrigation.

Monitoring Mechanism of the PMKSY

The programme will be supervised and monitored by the National Steering Committee under the chairmanship of Prime Minister with Union Ministers of all concerned Ministers. A National Executive Committee is to be constituted under the chairmanship of the vice chairman, NITI Aayog to oversee the programme Implementation, allocation of resources, inters ministerial coordination monitoring and performance assessment addressing administrative issues etc. At the state level the scheme is to be administered by a state level sanctioning committee to be chaired by the Chief Secretary of the respective states. The committee will have all authority to sanction the projects and also monitor the process of the scheme. At the district level there shall be a district level implementation committee for ensuring last mile coordination at the field level.

Conclusion

Agriculture is a biggest sector where 70 per cent people are engaged directly or indirectly for their livelihood. So there is a need for the rapid development of the sector. Irrigation is one of the most important measurements; which will be able to strengthen agriculture sector. At present 45 per cent cultivated land are out of the irrigation coverage. So it is very necessary to improve and expansion of this sector for the need of food for all. For the need of food security for each and every citizen; it is very necessary to increasing productivity of the food crops. For this aim government has taken initiative for another green revolution. For this revolution it is very necessary to strengthen irrigation system through renovation of traditional mood of irrigation system and expansion of existing system through more scientific eco-friendly ways. Coverage of total cultivated land under irrigation is very necessary task to the government for the internal security of citizen of India. The Pradhan Mantri Krishi Sinchayee

(PMKSY) is a strongest and suitable integrated inclusive irrigation plan of the present government which will be able to reach in dream of every Indian. It is one of the single integrated decentralized schemes, where provision has to renovation, improvement and expansion of irrigation system in India. Hope, it will be able to fill up the vision of the present government for agricultural sector 'Har Khet KO Pani' and 'Per Drop More Crop' slogan.

Pages: 145-154

Rural Economy: *Changing Landscape*
Edited by: **Dr. Kartick Das**
ISBN: 978-93-5056-838-5
Edition: **2017**
Published by: **Discovery Publishing House Pvt. Ltd., New Delhi (India)**

10 Facility of Primary Education in Birbhum District, West Bengal
A Geographical Interpretation

— **Debasis Ghosh** & **Mrinal Mandal**

INTRODUCTION

Education is one of the important instruments to enjoy a quality of life and freedom. The universal access to quality knowledge and skills ensures that every individual has an equal opportunity to play a significant role in work and society. The free and compulsory education up to the age of 14 is one of the fundamental rights of every citizen of the union as guaranteed by the constitution of India. (Mudaliar Commission Report, 1953, p. 04). National Policy of Education, 1986 stressed on radical reconstruction of education system, to improve its quality at all stages. According to Census of India 2001, 35 per cent of total population in the country was within the age of 14 years and this figure has not been changed drastically. The percentage should be considered as asset of the country not as number (Pratichi Institute, 2013, p. 04). During 1960's, education was considered as important factor for socio-economic development of society. But low income countries sensed it much later in 1980's, and in between this time some policies had already been adopted to invest more in education by other high income countries (Biswal, 2011, p. 1). The first evidence-based study for primary schooling quality in India was done by. The Public Report on Basic Education (PROBE Team, 1999). The study was based on 1996's survey of schooling facilities in 242 villages across five north Indian states, such as: Bihar, Madhya Pradesh, Rajasthan, Uttar Pradesh and Himachal Pradesh. Very poor infrastructure in schools was found by the PROBE, such as: lack of blackboard in every classroom, playground, drinking water, toilet, maps and charts, toys, library, musical instruments and so on (Kingdon, 2007, p. 16). Here an attempt has been made to investigate the status of primary education of Birbhum district considering three basic indicators.

Literature Review

There are several studies done by different scholars in many aspects of education. Some relevant works are referred here. In an article Kingdon, 2007 mentioned that India in compared to other countries of the world, the participation rate in primary school is lesser than youth literacy rate. According to ASER survey (Pratham, 2007), 93.4 per cent of Indian elementary school age children were enrolled in school in 2006. It was also stated China is more than thirty years ahead of India in terms of proportion of people completed secondary and post-secondary schooling (Kingdon, 2007, p. 3). According to the report of UNESCO, 2010, about 124.8 million illiterate people live in the developing countries (99.5% of the world), in which 40.4 million (32.2%) people belong to India. It is known to all that there is a huge gap in terms of income and socio-economic inequality in India and one out of ten children ages 6-10 is out of school (Biswal, 2011, pp. 3-4). The West Bengal Development Report, 2010 reported that in the state of West Bengal, the literacy rate of the people aged 7 years and above is higher than the national average. In contrast, during the 50th and 55th National Sample Survey rounds, growth rate of literacy was found to be lower at all India level. The report also talked about the female literacy rate, which is relatively progressing compared to national level and more interestingly the growth rate is observed in rural areas than in urban areas (Planning Commission, 2010, p. 130). India Human Development Report 2011: Towards Social Inclusion also argued the same in support of this report that the overall literacy rate of the country has increased and variation among the states in terms of literacy has also decreased in both rural and urban areas of India. The literacy rate is increasing higher in rural areas compared to urban areas. So, the gap between these areas will be reduced soon (Planning Commission, 2011, p. 13). In one study made by Mandal and Ganguli in Bankura district, where it was found that the status of primary education in the district was in moderate condition based on three basic parameters such as: TIR, ISR and TSR. (Mandal and Ganguli, 2011, p. 178).

There is no such relevant literature on primary education of Birbhum district which tries to explore the status of the primary education and how much variation exists in terms of educational facility among the blocks. Beside this, the closeness of the blocks to each other in respect to facility is identified. In this study we have set three objectives. *Firstly*, the study investigates the spatial distribution of educational facilities at primary level. *Secondly*, from the distribution of individual facility of educational system across the blocks, it is difficult to determine that the relative position of the block in terms of educational status. We have also developed a composite index of educational status of each block. *Thirdly*, the study assesses the nature of similarity of blocks in terms of the primary educational facility.

Materials and Methods

The study is based on secondary data which have been collected from District Statistical Handbook Birbhum, 2012. The district map of Birbhum has been collected from 18th All India Livestock Census, Agriculture Implements and Machinery, Fishery Statistics, West Bengal, 2007. Three main parameters have been adopted for this study namely: institution, student and teacher of primary school level of Birbhum district. All the urban (municipality) primary schools, teachers and students have been added up to their respective administrative block's primary schools, teachers and students. Here school has been termed as institution. Secondary data have been analysed to find out Teacher Institution Ratio (TIR), Institute Student Ratio (ISR) and Teacher Student Ratio (TSR) using following formulae.

$$TIR = \frac{Teacher}{Institution} \tag{1}$$

$$ISR = \frac{Institution \times 1000}{Students} \tag{2}$$

$$TSR = \frac{Teacher \times 1000}{Students} \tag{3}$$

In the second step we have computed TIR, ISR and TSR indices on the basis of mentioned three indicators namely: TIR, ISR and TSR. The calculated indicators are computed in Table 10.1.

Table 10.1: Indicators of Educational Facility and their Goalposts

Indicators	Goalpost of Indicators	
	Maximum Value	*Minimum Value*
TIR	4.299 (Murarai-II)	2.804 (Rajnagar)
ISR	16.183 (Rajnagar)	4.528 (Murarai-II)
TSR	45.383 (Rajnagar)	19.467 (Murarai-II)

Source: Authors' computation.

In order to construct the Primary Educational Facility Index (PEFI), we have computed indicator index for each indicator by the following formula.

$$I_i = \frac{A_i - m_i}{M_i - m_i} \tag{4}$$

Where; I_i = Indicator index of ith indicator, A_i = Actual value i^{th} of indicator, M_i = Maximum value i^{th} of indicator and m_i = Minimum value i^{th} of indicator.

On the basis of the indices of indicators, the actual position of the block in the three dimensional Cartesian space may be plotted by the vector (I_{1j}, I_{2j}, I_{3j}). The best situation, which is primary educational facility, can be found in Cartesian space vector in terms of (1, 1, 1). The worst primary educational facility is denoted by the vector (0, 0, 0). At the end the Primary Educational Facility Index (PEFI) has been computed measuring the normalized inverse Euclidian distance of the vector (I_{1j}, I_{2j}, I_{3j}) from the worst condition (0, 0, 0). Therefore, the following formula can be put here as the each indicator/parameter has been given same weightage.

$$PEFI = 1 - \sqrt{\frac{\sum_{t=1}^{3}(1-I_t)^2}{3}} \tag{5}$$

The normalization of Euclidian distance is done in order to ensure the range of PEFI from '0' to '1'. As the inverse distance has been taken, higher value of PEFI represents higher PEF. Thus the value '0' indicates no PEF and '1' indicates highest PEF. This distance-based approach has an advantage over the UNDP methodology of measuring achievement or deprivation Index. In UNDP methodology, the index presents the arithmetic or geometric average of the standardised indicators. It assumes perfect substitutability across the dimensions or indicators. Under this assumption a decrease in value of one indicator can be compensated by an increase of equal magnitude in another indicator.

Thus, if all dimensions or indicators are equally important for the all over index value the perfect substitutability among the indicators is an unrealistic assumption. In the distance based approach we do not need this unrealistic assumption. Our PEFI formula satisfies the properties of normalisation, symmetry, monotonicity, proximity, uniformity and signalling. But methodology of HDI follows only the properties *viz*; normalisation, symmetry, monotonicity. Thus, our distance based measure of PEF is superior to the measures based on UNDP methodology. This methodology is also applied in a study by Bagli and Adhikary, 2015 and Ghosh and Mandal, 2015. The PEFI varies from '0' to '1' where; the value '0' and '1' refers to perfect primary educational facility and worst primary educational facility respectively. To have the better understanding of PEFI of each block, the value of PEFI has been divided into five sub-ranges. The very good condition of PEFI is represented by $0.8<PEFI\leq1.0$ and good condition of PEF is indicated by $0.6<PEFI\leq0.8$. The range $0.4<PEFI\leq0.6$ refers the moderate condition of PEF and the poor condition is experienced by those blocks having the PEFI range of $0.2<PEFI\leq0.4$ and very poor condition is represented by the range of $0\leq PEFI\leq0.2$.

Ranking of the PEFI has been done (after Kendall's method) to identify the position of each block in the district. In order to investigate which blocks are close to each other based on TIR, ISR and TSR indicators, we have used the tool of cluster analysis (SPSS Software-20) following squared Euclidian distance method. Finally, to show the possible clusters of the blocks we have drawn the Dendrogram adopting average linkage method.

Study Area at a Glance

The geographical coordinates (District Statistical Handbook Birbhum, 2012, p. 1) of the Birbhum district are: 22°382 N86°362 E to 23°382 N 87°462 E (Fig. 10.1). It has an area of 4,545 km^2. The

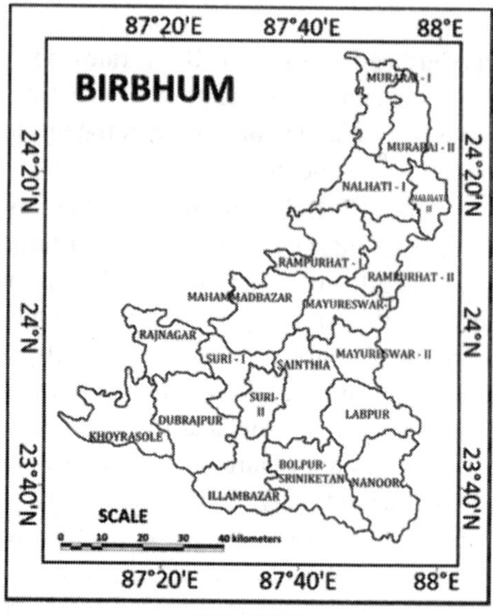

Fig. 10.1

population size and density of the district are 35,02,404 (Male - 51.13% and Female - 48.87%) and 771/km^2 respectively (Census of India, 2011). Total rural and urban populations are 87.17 per cent and 12.83 per cent respectively. The literacy rate of the district is 70.68 per cent in which male is 76.92 per cent and female is 64.14 per cent. Total number of blocks, police stations, municipalities and sub-divisions are 19,18,6 and 3 respectively (District Statistical Handbook Birbhum, 2012).

Results and Discussion

Teacher Institution Ratio (TIR)

The term Teacher Institution Ratio (TIR) is used to indicate number of teachers available per primary school. The higher TIR value (Index) indicates more number of teachers available in schools. Considering this parameter, Murarai-II block enjoys first position having four teachers per school. In contrast, Rajnagar is in the last position where two teachers are available per school. The rest of the blocks are in moderate condition.

Institution Student Ratio (ISR)

The parameter Institution Student Ratio (ISR) represents the number of primary schools available per thousand students. Based on this parameter, Rajnagar ranks the 1st position having sixteen institutions per thousand students. Murarai-II block stands last having four schools available per thousand students. The rest of the blocks enjoy six to eleven institutions per thousand students.

Teacher Student Ratio (TSR)

Teacher Student Ratio refers to number of teachers available per thousand students. The best education can be obtained if the TSR value is higher. It is found that Rajnagar block is in the first position having forty five teachers available per thousand students followed by Bolpur-Sriniketan (41) and Suri-I (40). The worst condition is observed in Murarai-II block where nineteen teachers available per thousand students followed by Murarai-I (21) and Nalhati-II (26) and rest of the blocks fall in moderate condition.

Table 10.2: Primary Educational Facility Index (PEFI) of Birbhum District, 2011-12

C.D. Block	HSEFI	Rank	Remarks
Nalhati-I	0.4313	10	Moderate
Nalhati-II	0.3462	17	Poor
Murarai-I	0.2040	18	Poor
Murarai-II	0.1835	19	Very Poor
Mayureswar-I	0.5281	5	Moderate
Mayureswar-II	0.5446	3	Moderate
Rampurhat-I	0.4848	7	Moderate
Rampurhat-II	0.4410	9	Moderate
Mohammad Bazar	0.4628	8	Moderate
Sainthia	0.5075	6	Moderate
Dubrajpur	0.4106	15	Moderate
Rajnagar	0.4228	12	Moderate
Suri-I	0.6588	2	Good
Suri-II	0.5290	4	Moderate
Khoyrasole	0.4163	14	Moderate
Bolpur-Sriniketan	0.6811	1	Good
Labhpur	0.4309	11	Moderate
Nanoor	0.4167	13	Moderate
Illambazar	0.3987	16	Poor

Source: Authors' computation.

Overall Position

It is clear from Table 10.2, Primary Educational Facility Index (PEFI) that there is not a single block in the district enjoying very good condition of PEF. Only two blocks namely: Bolpur-Sriniketan and Suri-I experience good condition. Thirteen blocks of the district are in moderate condition. In contrast, three blocks are in poor condition and only Murarai block experience the very poor condition. It can be said the overall condition of the blocks is average in terms of PEFI.

Table 10.3: Description of the Educational Facility Indicators of Birbhum District

Descriptive Statistics	TIR	ISR	TSR	PEFI
Mean	3.545	9.574	33.302	0.447
Median	3.469	9.980	33.040	0.431
S.D.	0.407	2.413	6.301	0.123
CV	11.466	25.199	18.920	27.54
Min	2.804	4.528	19.467	0.184
Max	4.299	16.183	45.383	0.681

Source: Authors' computation.

We find from Table 10.3 that in an average there are three teachers available per institution in the district and no such variation of this parameter is observed in the district. In an average nine schools are available per thousand students and maximum number of schools are sixteen. The range of this parameter is twelve which is not at all expected. The average number of teacher available per thousand students in the district is thirty three. In contrast the maximum value is 45 and range is twenty six. The PEFI is an important indicator to understand the actual status of primary education. We find that the average PEFI value of the district is 0.447 and maximum and minimum values are 0.681 and 0.184 respectively. The range value is 0.497. The PEFI is found to be consistent and reliable.

Cluster Analysis

The similarity among the blocks in terms of the multiple indicators of Primary Educational Facility (PEF) is not reflected by Primary Educational Facility Index (PEFI). To overcome this problem, we have done cluster analysis for the indicators of PEF following

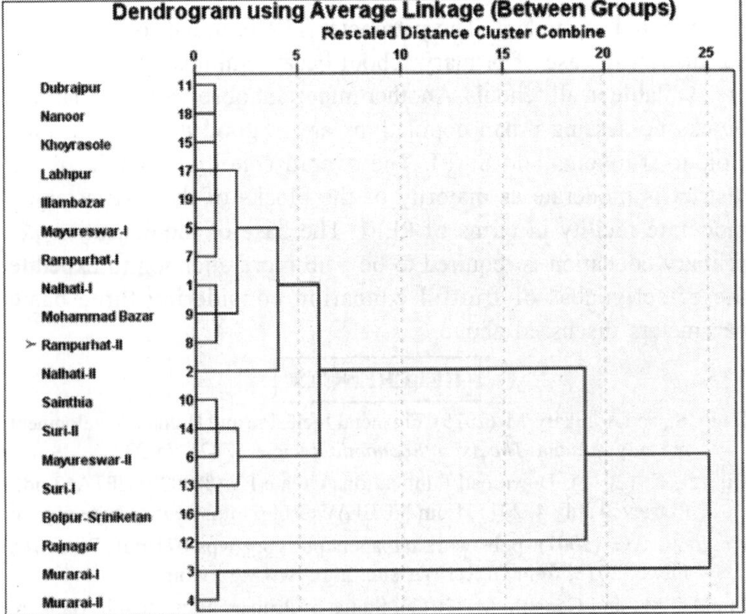

Fig. 10.2

specified methodology. The result of the cluster analysis is represented by the Dendrogram (Fig. 10.2). Here seven possible clusters have been identified from this analysis. The first cluster is consisted by Murarai-I and Murarai-II blocks. Rajnagar block makes a distinct cluster for it *i.e.,* second. Bolpur-Sriniketan and Suri-I blocks fall in the third cluster. Sainthia, Suri-II and Mayureswar-II blocks belong to fourth cluster. The fifth cluster is made by Nalhati-II block. In contrast, Nalhati-I, Mohammad Bazar and Rampurhat blocks fall in the sixth cluster. The rest of the blocks are in the last seventh cluster. If we consider 10 point scale of dissimilarity, we find except first and second clusters, rest of the five clusters fall in the same cluster.

Conclusion

At this end it is easy to understand that the average value of PEFI is 0.447 for the district, which is less than fifty per cent of highest value of PEFI *i.e.* We observe poor reflection of ISR and TSR indicators. There are some blocks having not a single school per hundred of student and some schools are having two teachers per hundred of student. The parameter TIR is found to be good in the district in case of primary school because almost three teachers are available in all schools. Another important observation is that few blocks possessing urban populations are in good position such as: Bolpur-Sriniketan and Suri-I. The overall condition of PEF of the district is moderate as majority of the blocks of the district enjoy moderate facility in terms of PEFI. The base of the education *i.e.* primary education is required to be paid more attention to expedite the effectiveness of fruitful education considering three basic parameters discussed above.

REFERENCES

Bagli, S., and Adhikary, M. (2015). Financial Inclusion and Human Development A Study in India. *The Asian Economic Review, 57* (2), 75-93.

Biswal, K. (2011). Download/Publications/Create/PTA%202011/PTA63.pdf. Retrieved July 4, 2015, from NUEPAWebsite: http://www.nuepa.org

Kingdon, G.G. (2007). pubs/workingpapers/pdf/gprg-wps-071-pdf. Retrieved July 5, 2015, from GPRG Website: http://www.gprg.org

Mandal, M., and Ganguli, M. (2011). Status of Primary Education in Bankura District, West Bengal: A Geographical Interpretation. *Indian Journal of Landscape Systems And Ecological Studies*, 34(1), 171-182.

Government of India (2011). *Census of India.* New Delhi: Directorate of Census.

Government of India (2011). *India Human development Report 2011: Towards Social Inclusion.* Institute of Applied Manpower Research. New Delhi: Planning Commission.

Government of India (2010). *West Bengal Development Report.* New Delhi: Planning Commission.

Government of India (1953). *Report of the Secondary Education Commission, Mudaliar Commission Report.* New Delhi: Ministry of Education.

Government of West Bengal (2014). *District Statistical Handbook, Birbhum 2012.* Kolkata: Bureau of Applied Economics and Statistics.

Government of West Bengal (2009). *District Statistical Handbook, Birbhum 2007.* Kolkata: Bureau of Applied Economics and Statistics.

Pratichi Institute (2013). *Secondary Education in West Bengal Prospect and Challenges.* Kolkata.

Index

H

I

J

K

L

M

R

S

T

U

W

Y

□□□